3-MINUTE
PRAYERS
for a
Less Stressed Life

Our mission is to inspire the world with the life-changing message of the Bible.

3-MINUTE PRAYERS

for a
Less Stressed Life

JANICE THOMPSON

BARBOUR
PUBLISHING

Introduction

Quiet down before GOD, be prayerful before him.
PSALM 37:7 MSG

. . . .

*L*ife can be stressful. There's no doubt about it. The world is a crazy, chaotic place, after all. Even the strongest believer can get worked up at times.

So how do you calm your spirit when things reach the boiling point? It's as easy as 1-2-3. Three minutes with Him can turn everything around.

These comforting prayers are especially for those days when you are mired in the stress of everyday life and your soul is longing for a quiet time of refreshment in the heavenly Creator's calming presence. Three minutes from your hectic day is all you need to fill your cup to overflowing with peace for life's journey.

- Minute 1: Read and reflect on God's Word.
- Minute 2: Pray, using the provided prayer to jump-start a conversation with God.
- Minute 3: Reflect on a question for further thought.

Although this book isn't meant as a tool for deep Bible study, each calming prayer can be a touchstone to keep you grounded and focused on the One who hears all your prayers. May this book remind you that the heavenly Father cares about everything you have to say. Go on. . .talk to Him today. He's ready and waiting to hear from you!

Anxious for Nothing

Do not be anxious about anything, but in everything by prayer and supplication with thanksgiving let your requests be made known to God. And the peace of God, which surpasses all understanding, will guard your hearts and your minds in Christ Jesus.

PHILIPPIANS 4:6–7 ESV

Lord, sometimes I get so wound up! I'm like a ticking bomb, about to go off. Stresses add up, one on top of the other, and I don't always handle them the way I should. Then I'm reminded of Your Word: "Do not be anxious about anything."

You have a great plan to turn things around, but it requires action on my part. You want to involve me in the process. So here I am, Father, pouring out my supplications with thanksgiving in my heart because I know You'll answer my prayers when and how You choose. My choice, Lord, is to trust You in the process. Thanks for loving me enough to care about my anxieties! I'm so grateful, Father. Amen.

How do you turn your anxiety around?

He Will Deliver Me

Moses answered the people, "Do not be afraid. Stand
firm and you will see the deliverance the LORD will bring
you today. The Egyptians you see today you will never see
again. The LORD will fight for you; you need only to be still."
EXODUS 14:13–14 NIV

Lord, I'll be honest—there are days when I'm so stressed out, I can't think straight. On those days, it's like I forget who You are and what You're capable of. I'm overwhelmed by my circumstances, unable to see past them.

Then I'm reminded of this story from Your Word. If You could deliver the Israelites from the hands of their enemies, surely You have me covered as well. So I won't stress out. I'll stand firm just as You asked them to do. And I know that I will see deliverance just as they did. How I praise You for Your supernatural intervention, Lord! Amen.

Can you remember a specific time when
God intervened in your situation?

Even When I Can't See It

*Now faith is confidence in what we hope for
and assurance about what we do not see.*

HEBREWS 11:1 NIV

I'm one of those "see it to believe it" types, Lord. Then again, You already know this about me. Many times I've needed a faith boost, especially when my physical eyes couldn't see what You were up to.

You're teaching me that I can trust You even when I don't see what's coming around the bend. You've never let me down, and You're not going to start now. So I will choose to let You lead the way, no matter how blurry the picture looks. I love You and I trust You, Lord. Amen.

*When was the last time you had to
lean on your faith in a major way?*

The God of Peace

May the God of peace be with you all. Amen.
ROMANS 15:33 ESV

I turn on the evening news and get overwhelmed, Lord! Then I get a text from a friend who's going through a crisis, followed by a call that a loved one has been diagnosed with cancer.

There are times when it feels like it's all too much to handle. The stresses of life reach a tipping point, and peace flies right out the window. Then, in heavenly fashion, You sweep in. Somehow You calm the storm. You make a way where there seemed to be no way. Your Spirit hovers over me, bringing peace like a warm, cozy blanket on a cold day.

I never want to forget that true peace is found only in You, Lord. You are truly the God of peace, and I am forever grateful. Amen.

Have you ever sensed God's presence
in the middle of a difficult season?

No Matter What. . .He's There

"When you pass through the waters, I will be with you; and through the rivers, they shall not overwhelm you; when you walk through fire you shall not be burned, and the flame shall not consume you."
ISAIAH 43:2 ESV

I've been through seasons, Lord, when I felt like I was going to drown. I was up to my eyeballs in chaos and confusion—at work, at home, even with the kids or other loved ones. Yet somehow I managed to stay afloat. I haven't drowned yet, and I believe You'll be there to pull me out of the depths of the water again and again.

Thank You for saving me, and thank You for the way You intervene. You're always there, right when I need rescuing. (You're the best Lifeguard out there, Lord!)

I won't be overwhelmed. I won't be overtaken. I will trust You even when I pass through deep waters. Amen.

How did God prove Himself strong during your last flood or fire season?

I'm an Overcomer!

*For everyone who has been born of God overcomes
the world. And this is the victory that has overcome
the world—our faith. Who is it that overcomes the world
except the one who believes that Jesus is the Son of God?*

1 JOHN 5:4–5 ESV

I'm so grateful for the reminder that I'm an overcomer,
Lord! I'm not ruled by my circumstances or feelings. I
don't have to give in to fear. I can—and will—have victory in
You, even when it feels impossible.

You've overcome sin, death, and the grave. You rose
again to new life, and You've given me the power to rise as
well—from my past, from my present, and from the problems
that seem to plague me.

Have I mentioned I'm grateful for the power You've given
me, Father? I am! I lift up praise to You, the One who brings
the victory. Amen.

*How can you remind yourself daily that you are
an overcomer and that stress doesn't rule you?*

Get Back Up Again

The godly may trip seven times, but they will get up again.
But one disaster is enough to overthrow the wicked.

PROVERBS 24:16 NLT

. . . .

I fall down, I get up. I fall down again, I get up again. Over and over this cycle goes.

Oh, I'm not complaining, Lord! Not at all. I'm so grateful You're there to pick me up again. If not for You, I'd still be down after my first tumble. But You won't let that happen. Whenever I trip, You catch me in Your arms and set my feet on solid ground again. How grateful I am for Your strong arms!

Your people are blessed, for You provide a supernatural safety net, one the ungodly don't possess. I'm glad I'm one of Your own, Father! Amen.

. . . .

How do you pick yourself up after you've fallen?

I Can Walk on Water!

*"Lord, if it's you," Peter replied, "tell me to come
to you on the water." "Come," he said. Then Peter
got down out of the boat, walked on the water and
came toward Jesus. But when he saw the wind, he was
afraid and, beginning to sink, cried out, "Lord, save me!"
Immediately Jesus reached out his hand and caught
him. "You of little faith," he said, "why did you doubt?"*

MATTHEW 14:28–31 NIV

. . . .

I love this story, Lord! You called out to Peter, and he
walked on the water. When he took his eyes off You, he
started to sink. Then, just as quickly, he looked Your way
and was saved.

I've been there more times than I can count. I was at
the near-sinking point; then I shifted my gaze to You and
bounced back up again. Thank You for meeting me, even
on tumultuous seas, Lord. Amen.

. . . .

*Can you think of a time when God
proved Himself in spite of your doubt?*

As You Say

Mary said, "I am the servant of the Lord. Let this happen to me as you say!" Then the angel went away.

Luke 1:38 NCV

• •

Lord, I love the story of how Mary submitted herself to Your authority. She spoke the words, "As You say." They serve as a reminder that Your way is higher. Your way is wiser.

I'm facing a lot of chaos in my life. I want things the way I want them. But Mary's story also reminds me that I'm not really in charge of my own life. You are. And if she could trust You, I can too. So I'll say the words that she spoke: "As You say, Lord."

As You say in my relationships. As You say in my work. As You say in my provision. As You say in my hopes and dreams. Your way is better. As You say. Amen.

• •

Can you think of a time when you preferred to do things your way and not God's? Did your way lead to peace or stress?

Fiery Trials

Shadrach, Meshach, and Abednego answered and said to the king, "O Nebuchadnezzar, we have no need to answer you in this matter. If this be so, our God whom we serve is able to deliver us from the burning fiery furnace, and he will deliver us out of your hand, O king. But if not, be it known to you, O king, that we will not serve your gods or worship the golden image that you have set up."

DANIEL 3:16–18 ESV

. . . .

I know You never promised me a fire-free journey, Lord. But this story of Shadrach, Meshach, and Abednego is a great reminder that even in the most fiery trials, You're right there in the midst of the flames.

Sometimes I feel like I'll be consumed, if I'm being honest. But You saved these three Hebrew men who put their trust in You, and You'll save me too. No stress, no problem, no heartache is so big that You can't pull me out of it. Thank You for delivering me, Lord! Amen.

. . . .

Do you believe God is able to deliver you from impossible situations?

Blessed with Peace (Not Stress!)

The LORD gives strength to his people;
the LORD blesses his people with peace.
PSALM 29:11 NIV

*W*hen I think of all the gifts my parents passed down, I'm so grateful. And when I think of all the gifts that You, my heavenly Father, have passed down. . .I get even more excited!

You give me things like hope, joy, and peace. Every gift is life-giving. So when I'm feeling stressed? When I'm feeling overwhelmed? Those feelings aren't from you. They're definitely not gifts! Usually, they've come because I'm in over my head.

But You, Lord, offer the gift of peace even in situations that feel overwhelming! And with that peace comes great strength. Oh, how I appreciate that strength on the rough days! Amen.

When was the last time God gave you
strength and peace in place of your anxiety?

Rejoicing in Tribulations

Hannah prayed and said, "My heart exults in the LORD;
my horn is exalted in the LORD. My mouth derides
my enemies, because I rejoice in your salvation."
1 SAMUEL 2:1 ESV

• •

I love the story of Hannah, Lord. Even in her tribulations, as she waited and prayed for a child, she never gave up. And when You finally answered her prayer and gave her a son, Samuel, she was quick to praise You.

I want to live my life that way! Even in times of tribulation, may I lift my voice to You. Even when things look bleak, may I place my trust in You. You have always come through for me, Lord. I know You won't fail me now. I want to be a Hannah—faithful until I see the promise fulfilled. Help me, I pray. Amen.

• •

Did you stop to praise God the last
time He came through for you?

All of My Anxieties

Casting all your anxieties on him, because he cares for you.

1 PETER 5:7 ESV

*Y*ou ask me to cast all of my anxieties on You, Lord. To release them from my tight grip and toss them all the way to Your loving hands. No one else I know would make an offer like that. Who in the world would want to carry all of my burdens, especially with the stress I've been under lately? No one!

But You? You're not only willing but *able* to carry them all. And You desire to lift these burdens from me because You care so deeply for me. Your love means everything to me, Father. Thank You for reminding me I don't have to bear my problems alone. Amen.

Casting is a fishing term. When was the last time you "cast" your cares on the Lord?

Things Not Seen

*Now faith is the assurance of things hoped
for, the conviction of things not seen.*

HEBREWS 11:1 ESV

When I'm going through a stressful season, Lord, it's almost as if I'm staggering around in a dark room. I keep waiting for someone to turn on the lights, but it doesn't happen. Darkness surrounds me. In my imagination, the stresses will disappear when I'm able to see things more clearly.

You have a different way of seeing things. You're asking for my faith right now, right here, even in the middle of these stressful circumstances. Even when I can't see what's coming and don't know how to find my way out of this situation. Give me that kind of faith, I pray! I want the assurance of things I haven't yet seen, things I'm hoping for. Amen.

What things are you hoping for but haven't seen yet?

No Reason to Fear

*Fear not, for I am with you; be not dismayed, for I
am your God; I will strengthen you, I will help you,
I will uphold you with my righteous right hand.*

ISAIAH 41:10 ESV

. . . .

I'll admit it, Lord. Most of my stresses come from taking my eyes off You. When I begin to look in other directions, I get overwhelmed. I forget where my help comes from. Fear creeps in. It wriggles its way up my spine and hijacks my thoughts.

You are calling me to take anxious thoughts captive and to give my fears to You. Today I choose to lay my burdens at Your feet, heavenly Father. I'm counting on Your help to overcome my worry and angst. Amen.

. . . .

Is your stress triggered by fear?

A Good Word

Anxiety in a man's heart weighs him down,
but a good word makes him glad.
PROVERBS 12:25 ESV

....

I've been there so many times, Lord. Anxious. Bound up. Heavyhearted. Weighed down by the cares of life. Then, in the middle of it all, I turn to Your Word, and what a good word it is! With just a whisper from You, a frown can turn upside down. It sounds cliché, but it's true. You take my stresses and give me peace. You take my anger and give me joy.

Your Word is powerful, it's effective, and it brings lasting change. May I speak Your words over my situation, my relationships, and those I love. Amen.

....

What was the last "good word" someone offered you?

A Tree Planted by the Water

"Blessed is the man who trusts in the LORD, whose trust is the LORD. He is like a tree planted by water, that sends out its roots by the stream, and does not fear when heat comes, for its leaves remain green, and is not anxious in the year of drought, for it does not cease to bear fruit."
JEREMIAH 17:7–8 ESV

I want to be like that tree standing by the water, Lord. I want my roots to go down so deep that strong winds can't possibly blow me over. I don't want to be wobbly when stresses come. I want my leaves to remain green because I'm being fed and watered by You. I can only flourish when my roots run deep.

Thank You for removing my worry and anxiety, Lord. May this tree never cease to bear good fruit. Amen.

Are your leaves currently green?

No Traps for Me!

The fear of man lays a snare,
but whoever trusts in the LORD is safe.

PROVERBS 29:25 ESV

My emotions go up and down a lot, Lord! I go in and out of stressful seasons like some people go through a revolving door. I'm fickle at times, like a mouse chasing after elusive bits of cheese, not realizing he's about to be caught in a trap.

I know You're not the one who lays these traps, hoping to catch me off guard. The enemy of my soul places snares in my path. But I'm on to him! I will be more cautious. I know things can go poorly when I feel trapped and unsafe, so I will avoid his snares at every cost and put my trust in You! Amen.

How do you tend to respond when you feel trapped?

My Spiritual Worship

*I appeal to you therefore, brothers, by the
mercies of God, to present your bodies as
a living sacrifice, holy and acceptable to
God, which is your spiritual worship.*

ROMANS 12:1 ESV

• •

*Y*ou've asked me to present my body as a living sacrifice,
Lord. I've often wondered what that means. Are You
after my health? My thoughts? My attitude? Do you want to
change my outlook? My chubby thighs? My stubbornness?

Perhaps You're after all these things. When I offer You my
body as a living sacrifice, I give You all it contains—physically,
emotionally, and spiritually. Only then are You able to do
a complete work in me. I hold nothing back today. Amen.

• •

*What image does the phrase
"present your bodies" bring to mind?*

He's Never Far Away

When the righteous cry for help, the LORD hears and delivers them out of all their troubles. The LORD is near to the brokenhearted and saves the crushed in spirit.

PSALM 34:17–18 ESV

· ·

*Y*ou're not going anywhere, Lord. You've never left me, and You never will. When I cry out for help, You are right there, already at my side. You hear me. Even if I whisper a prayer, You don't miss a word. Best of all, You intervene! You deliver me from all my troubles.

Your nearness brings me hope, reminding me I don't have to walk alone during stressful seasons. I'll keep my eyes on You and remember that You're ready, willing, and able to deliver me, if only I call. Amen.

· ·

Do you sense God's nearness when you're in the middle of a stressful situation, or do you tend to push thoughts of Him aside?

Even When I Feel Like I Can't

I can do all things through him who strengthens me.
PHILIPPIANS 4:13 ESV

. . . .

*H*ere's the thing, Lord: I know I can't. By myself, I really can't. I know because I've tried in my own strength so many times and failed. But when I go to You, when I count on You to strengthen me from the inside out and give me the wisdom only You can give. . .then I can.

It's not me; it's You. I recognize that. From now on, please help me to recognize it before I waste precious time trying to be a superhero on my own. I won't attempt to go it alone anymore, Father. When I do, I always end up exhausted, afraid, and stressed out. I'm so glad You're ready to do the heavy lifting, Lord. Amen.

. . . .

How often do you use the word can't?

He Will Show Me Compassion

Yet the LORD longs to be gracious to you; therefore he will rise up to show you compassion. For the LORD is a God of justice. Blessed are all who wait for him!
ISAIAH 30:18 NIV

I blew it again, Lord. You were a firsthand witness to my catastrophe. Now I'm paying the price. Now the stresses of what I've caused are adding up and spilling over. What a fiasco.

But You? You're not mad at me. You're not pointing the finger and saying, "Good grief! What have you done?" No, You're right here, forgiving, loving, and encouraging me. . . as always. Give me that same compassionate heart toward others, I pray. May I learn to be gracious with others just as You have been with me. Amen.

Does the idea of "waiting" on God cause more stress for you or does it bring peace?

His Burden Is Light

"Come to me, all who labor and are heavy laden, and I will give you rest. Take my yoke upon you, and learn from me, for I am gentle and lowly in heart, and you will find rest for your souls. For my yoke is easy, and my burden is light."
MATTHEW 11:28–30 ESV

I love your swap plan, Lord. I give You chaos, You give me peace. I give You turmoil, You give me comfort. I give You heaviness, You give me featherlight freedom.

You ask me to take Your yoke upon me. That sounds heavy at first, but I've learned that Your yoke isn't weighty at all! It's freedom. It's joy. It's abundance. It's peace. It's the very opposite of what the world can give.

Today I celebrate the "burden" You ask me to carry. In You I find answers to every problem I could ever face. How grateful I am to be free, Lord. I'll rest easy in You. Amen!

When was the last time you truly rested in the Lord?

Why? Because You Care for Me!

Humble yourselves, therefore, under the mighty hand of God so that at the proper time he may exalt you, casting all your anxieties on him, because he cares for you.

1 PETER 5:6-7 ESV

Sometimes I feel like no one notices me. In fact, sometimes I wonder if anyone cares at all. I go through deep valleys, and no one seems to notice or respond to the pain I'm in. I realize that You do, of course! You notice. You care. You're right beside me, ready to lift me up when I'm down.

During those low seasons, You ask me to humble myself so that You can lift me up. I'll confess, I often don't feel like doing that. Things are tough enough already, and humility doesn't come naturally. But today I choose to humble myself in obedience, knowing You will bless me as I lay my whole life before You. Thank You for loving me! Amen.

Does humility come naturally to you?

I'm Not Getting Any Younger

*"And which of you by being anxious can
add a single hour to his span of life?"*
<small>MATTHEW 6:27 ESV</small>

Worry, worry, worry. Anxiety, anxiety, anxiety. Stress, stress, stress. It's a vicious cycle, Lord! I get worried, and then I panic. With panic comes fear. With fear comes doubt. With doubt comes a lack of faith. Finally, a lack of faith leads to hopelessness.

You have a better way, one meant to add years to my life. Give up the worry! Hand it over to You. I like this plan, Lord. I'm not getting any younger, after all. I need all the days (and hours) I can get, so I'll pass my troubles to You and age well. May my life span be free of anxiety as I put my hope in You! Amen.

*When you consider the notion that stress can shorten
your life, do you want to do a better job dealing with it?*

I Can't Run Away

But Jonah ran away from the Lord and headed for
Tarshish. He went down to Joppa, where he found a
ship bound for that port. After paying the fare, he went
aboard and sailed for Tarshish to flee from the Lord.

JONAH 1:3 NIV

H ow many times have I tried to run, Lord? A hundred?
Two? I'm a flight risk for sure! Troubles come, and I'm
out the door, headed for safety.

Only safety can never be found out there. I'm only safe
when I turn to You. Lesson learned. (The hard way, at times!)
I don't want to be a Jonah. When You call, I want to respond
with "Yes, Lord," even when it's hard. Really, really hard.

Stresses come when I say no to You. So today I say yes
to Your call, Your plan, Your way. Thank You for holding tight
to me, especially when I'm tempted to run. Amen.

When was the last time you tried to run away
from a problem? How did that story end?

An Untroubled Heart

"Let not your hearts be troubled.
Believe in God; believe also in me."

JOHN 14:1 ESV

There are days, Lord, when things just feel off. I can't quite put my finger on what's wrong, but I feel troubled deep down in my soul. I'm unsettled. Fretful. Worried without any logical reason. This verse reminds me that I can have an untroubled heart. That nagging sensation has to leave when I invite You into the picture.

Today I invite You into my emotions. Into my pain. Into my stress. Into my troubles. You're right there, standing at my heart's door, knocking. I swing wide the gate and say, "Yes, Lord! Come on in and take control." What a relief to give this troubled heart to You! You handle it with great care, and I'm so grateful. Amen.

When you hear the phrase "troubled
heart," what images come to mind?

I Won't Worry about Tomorrow

"But seek first the kingdom of God and his righteousness, and all these things will be added to you. Therefore do not be anxious about tomorrow, for tomorrow will be anxious for itself. Sufficient for the day is its own trouble."

MATTHEW 6:33-34 ESV

Why do I worry about tomorrow, Lord? It's not even here yet! I have enough to deal with today without fretting over tomorrow and the days after that.

And yet I still struggle with fear regarding the unknown. I know—deep in the recesses of my heart—that the only way out of this fear is to give my tomorrows to You. I've trusted You with my yesterdays, and You've always come through. I trust You with today and sense Your presence. Why, then, would I give up on tomorrow before it even arrives?

I won't. I look forward with anticipation and hope, not fear. Thank You for joining me in my tomorrows, Father! Amen.

What actions can you take to avoid worrying about things that haven't happened yet?

You Bind My Wounds

He heals the brokenhearted and binds up their wounds.
PSALM 147:3 ESV

Sometimes I feel like my heart has a gaping wound, Lord. If You didn't reach down and bind it, I might bleed out. The cruel words spoken over me, the ugly actions of others, even my own self-loathing. . .they've done a number on me.

I'm so grateful for your TLC in moments like these. You're like a paramedic, reaching down to put pressure on the wound to keep it from depleting me. Then You supernaturally infuse me with Your blood, Your power, Your joy. And somehow—in spite of the pain and trials—I keep going. The wound doesn't take me down. You cure me and set me aright, healthy and whole. Thank You for such great care, heavenly Father. How tenderly You treat this heart of mine! I'm so grateful. Amen.

What specific wounds from your past has God healed?

A Parting Gift

"Peace I leave with you; my peace I give to you.
Not as the world gives do I give to you. Let not
your hearts be troubled, neither let them be afraid."
JOHN 14:27 ESV

Lord, I love this verse! Your parting gift to Your followers was peace. Peace to have faith for the things we cannot see. Peace to overcome obstacles. Peace to take the place of turmoil.

It's Your peace, Jesus. As I pause to think it through, I realize this peace passed through Your hands before landing in mine. You don't give me the world's version, filtered through modern-day culture. No, You breathe on it and then pass it directly to me so that my heart and life can be permanently changed.

"Let not your hearts be troubled." Oh, how I love those words! The Savior of the world loves me so much that He left me this amazing parting gift. I'll take it. Apply it. Live it. Thank You, Lord! Amen.

What do you suppose Jesus meant when He
added, "Not as the world gives do I give to you"?

A Quiet, Peaceful Place

The LORD is my shepherd; I shall not want. He makes me lie down in green pastures. He leads me beside still waters.

PSALM 23:1–2 ESV

*Y*ou make me lie down in green pastures. I'll admit, there are times when I don't want to. I want to keep going, going, going. . .until my body and my will give out. But You? You know better. So You lead me to quiet streams with shade trees nearby. You woo me with Your gentle words, encouraging me to rest. To relax. To be with You.

When I take the time to enjoy the stillness with You, the stresses of life have no choice but to flee! So today I choose still waters over chaos. I choose shade trees over the beating sun. I choose peace over turmoil. And I choose You over me. Thank You for leading me beside still waters, Lord. Amen.

*How has God "made you" lie down
in green pastures in the past?*

All Things Are Possible

"For nothing will be impossible with God."
LUKE 1:37 ESV

· ·

*I*f I'm being honest, Lord, I have to confess that I haven't always believed You to be capable of "all" things. There were certain things—people, relationships, situations—that I gave up on. I just couldn't see it happening, so I didn't bother asking You to intervene. Or maybe I asked but then quickly gave up.

I see now the futility of my approach. You wanted to be free to move on my behalf, but I limited You. I said, "Never mind that person, Lord. She's never going to change." Today I ask for Your intervention in the situations that seem impossible to me. May I watch the impossible change to possible once You take the reins! Amen.

· ·

Do you have faith to believe that "all" things are possible?

He Fights My Enemies

David said to the Philistine, "You come against me
with sword and spear and javelin, but I come against
you in the name of the LORD Almighty, the God of
the armies of Israel, whom you have defied."
1 SAMUEL 17:45 NIV

. . . .

Oh, how I love David's bold words in today's scripture, Lord! How dare that evil giant think he stood a chance against a man of God! How dare he lift his sword and spear to take down one of God's anointed!

You've got our backs, Lord—even when we face strong (giant!) opposition. Even then we come out swinging—not with weapons of warfare like the world uses, but in Your name. We come against the forces of darkness in the name of the Lord Almighty, the God of the armies of Israel. When those who speak against God rear their heads, we take them down with smooth stones, not earthly weapons. And we do it with Your power, Your strength, and Your confidence. Thank You for making us battle ready, Lord. Amen.

. . . .

How can you hand the reins over to the Lord
today so that your stresses can be relieved?

Getting Out of My Head

*Trust in the LORD with all your heart, and do not
lean on your own understanding. In all your ways
acknowledge him, and he will make straight your paths.*
PROVERBS 3:5-6 ESV

It's so hard to get out of my head most of the time, Lord. I get wrapped up in my thoughts, my plans, my worries, my vain imaginings, and I forget to put my trust in You. I wonder why I end up with my stomach in knots and my hands trembling. It's because I tried to take Your place.

Today I give my thoughts, my worries, my anxieties to You. I won't lean on my own understanding. (This is going to be hard for me, but You already know that!) I'll stop, take a breath, and acknowledge Your rightful place as the Solver of all my problems. And when I do, I know You'll straighten my path and show me which way to go.

Whew! I'm so glad I can trust You, Father! Amen.

*What are some techniques you can use to
get out of your head and trust God more?*

When My Knees Are Knocking

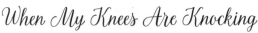

"Be strong and courageous. Do not fear or be in dread of them, for it is the LORD your God who goes with you. He will not leave you or forsake you."

DEUTERONOMY 31:6 ESV

"Do not fear or be in dread." I read those words in today's verse and want to ask, "How do I *do* that, Lord? When I'm totally stressed out—when things are going the very opposite of how I hoped they would go—how do I keep from becoming fearful? How can I push away dread, especially when the enemy is taunting or intimidating me?

Then I read the rest of this verse and get my answer. You're going with me. Whew! You're right beside me. You won't leave, no matter how heated the battle gets. In fact, the tougher the battle, the tighter You stick to me. I'll trust You, Lord. Even in the battle. *Especially* in the battle. Amen.

Are you easily intimidated?

Every Need. . .Met!

*And my God will supply every need of yours
according to his riches in glory in Christ Jesus.*
PHILIPPIANS 4:19 ESV

Okay, I'll admit it—sometimes I get worried and worked up over things that haven't even happened yet. A bill comes in the mail, and I panic without even considering how You will make provision. I get totally stressed out and ignore Your gentle reminder: *"Hey, haven't I taken care of every single need in the past? Do you really think I'm going to start letting you down now?"*

I know You won't, Lord. You're a Way Maker. You're a Need Meeter. You supply every good thing for those who love you and are called according to Your purpose. I trust You, Father, even when the need seems great. Amen.

*What (particular) needs are you
praying God will supply today?*

Even Then. . .

*Even though I walk through the valley of the
shadow of death, I will fear no evil, for you are
with me; your rod and your staff, they comfort me.*
PSALM 23:4 ESV

We've been through some hard seasons, You and me.
I've trudged through valleys so deep, so dark, that I
questioned Your existence. I've been on seas so turbulent
that I felt sure I wouldn't pull through.

But You. . . Even then, in the midst of the despair, You
always showed up and showed off! I don't have to be afraid
because I've seen You intervene in the past and I know
You'll do it again. And again. And again. Even when things
are at their worst, I can trust You. Today I choose to do just
that. Amen.

How are you comforted by God's rod and staff?

You've Been There, Lord

*And Jesus, full of the Holy Spirit, returned from the Jordan
and was led by the Spirit in the wilderness for forty days,
being tempted by the devil. And he ate nothing during
those days. And when they were ended, he was hungry.*

LUKE 4:1–2 ESV

*K*nowing You've walked a mile in my shoes brings
me so much hope, Lord. You understand what it's
like to be tempted. You know how it feels to be in pain.
You've experienced betrayal, anger, and frustration too. You've
been hungry. And thirsty. And weary. And yet—through the
power of Your Spirit—You overcame it all.

You're teaching me to overcome too. Help me to lean into
You on days when I'm feeling weak. Even when I'm feeling
strong, I want to fully rely on You. Thank You for leading
the way. Amen.

*How do you feel knowing that Jesus
has walked a mile in your shoes?*

Ruling in my Heart

*And let the peace of Christ rule in your hearts, to which
indeed you were called in one body. And be thankful.*

COLOSSIANS 3:15 ESV

I have to confess, I've been ruled by many things over the years, Lord. My temper. My poor attitude. My jealousy. My frustration. These and other things have taken control of my heart at different times, and poor actions always followed.

But no more! Now I'm ruled by Your peace. I'm giving it first place in my heart. I'm so thankful for Your supernatural peace because I know it will affect my actions, and others will notice. And once they see the change in me, I'll be able to share more freely about all You're doing in my life. Being ruled by peace is a beautiful cycle! I'm so grateful I can live this way. Amen.

What does it mean to be ruled by peace?

No Fear in Love

*There is no fear in love, but perfect love casts
out fear. For fear has to do with punishment,
and whoever fears has not been perfected in love.*

1 JOHN 4:18 ESV

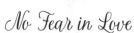

J read this verse, Lord, and I'm mesmerized. I'm trying to
figure out how to get rid of the fear and anxiety in my life,
and the answer is right in front of me—love. When I'm fully
convinced of Your great love for me, when I'm overwhelmed
by Your grace, no room is left for fear or stress.

Consume me with Your love and grace today, I pray. Take
hold of those things that trouble me most deeply. Wash away
my fears with Your peace. Remove angst. Leave behind only
joy, flowing from the wellspring of Your Spirit. I give myself
over to this way of living, Lord. Thank You for providing a
way out of stress. Amen.

What do fear and love have to do with each other?

Get Over It!

Refrain from anger, and forsake wrath!
Fret not yourself; it tends only to evil.

PSALM 37:8 ESV

· ·

*Y*ou ask me to forsake wrath, Lord. But forsaking wrath isn't as easy as it sounds. More often than not, I lose it! Oh, I never mean to. It always seems to hit from out of the blue. Someone gets on my last nerve, and I come out swinging, exhibiting the very opposite of this verse: I'm angry. Filled with wrath. Fretting. And in those moments, I really do have a propensity toward evil.

But You have a different way. What a relief to know there's a way out. Today I swap out anger and wrath for God-breathed peace. I trade in my fretting for trust. And I turn my back on evil, refusing to give the enemy a foothold in my life.

Thank You for giving Your children a better way, Lord. Amen.

· ·

Are you one of those people who has
a hard time "getting over" things?

Because I Trust in You

*You keep him in perfect peace whose mind
is stayed on you, because he trusts in you.*
ISAIAH 26:3 ESV

Sometimes I wonder what "perfect" peace looks like. Is it mountain streams or ocean waves? Is it a baby's coo or a puppy's cuddles? Is it a cozy blanket and a cup of tea on a cold day?

You show up with feelings of peace in all sorts of ways, Father God, but by far Your best offering came through the sacrifice of Your Son, Jesus, on the cross. Because of Your amazing gift, I can have lasting peace to carry me through not just the situations I'm facing today but all of the stresses of tomorrow.

The world can't give this peace to me, and no circumstances are strong enough to take it away. Perfect peace comes through the blood of Jesus, the One who cleansed me from my sin and set my feet on a rock. How grateful I am for this overcoming peace! Amen.

What do the words "perfect peace" mean to you?

Knees. . .Stop Knocking!

*"Have I not commanded you? Be strong and courageous.
Do not be frightened, and do not be dismayed, for
the LORD your God is with you wherever you go."*

JOSHUA 1:9 ESV

I'm noticing a cycle, Lord. My most stressful moments come when I forget to place my trust in You. I panic, and then fear sets in. But You've commanded me to be strong. I think it's a little sad that You have to command this—courage should come naturally to me, but it doesn't.

I take Your commands seriously, Lord. You obviously care a great deal about courage if You commanded it! "Do not be frightened" is easier said than done. "Do not be dismayed"? Only possible through You, Lord!

Here's my favorite part of that verse: "For the LORD your God is with you wherever you go." And that, of course, is the answer to how and why it is possible to rise above fear. Thank You, Lord! Amen.

*Why do you suppose God made courage
a command instead of a suggestion?*

I'm Tossing It Your Way, Lord!

*Cast your burden on the LORD, and he will sustain
you; he will never permit the righteous to be moved.*
PSALM 55:22 ESV

When I think of how You sustain me, Lord, I imagine a net holding me above my troubles. You lift me out of them in much the same way a mother scoops her child into her arms. It's easy to cast my burden on you when I picture You holding me like that. You care—about my chaos, my confusion, my struggles, my pain. And because You care, you sustain. (That safety net is there anytime I need it.)

The word *sustain* gives me courage to look ahead. If You're willing to sustain me today, I can count on it tomorrow too. Thanks for giving me a way to rise above my problems, Lord. Amen.

In what ways has God sustained you this week?

A Fixed Mind

You keep him in perfect peace whose mind
is stayed on you, because he trusts in you.
ISAIAH 26:3 ESV

Today I choose to fix my mind on You, Lord. I'm tempted to look to the right. No, I'm tempted to look to the left. I'm tempted to look every way the wind blows if I'm being honest. Distractions beckon. Temptations abound. They cry out for my attention, but I'm not falling into their trap! I've done that before, and things didn't end well.

This time things *will* end well because I've made up my mind to keep my heart, my thoughts, and my attitude firmly fixed on You—Your Word, Your plan, Your way. I won't give up if things don't come together instantly. I'll stick with You. You've stuck with me, after all. (Have I mentioned how grateful I am for that, Lord?) Amen.

What does it mean to "fix" your mind?

You Started It, You'll Finish It

And I am sure of this, that he who began a good work in you will bring it to completion at the day of Jesus Christ.

PHILIPPIANS 1:6 ESV

I don't always finish what I start, do I, Lord? It's a real problem. I'll come up with a craft project or redecorating scheme on a whim. Things get off to a great start, but then my ambition fizzles out. I get stuck. I give up. I leave rooms half finished.

You, though? You don't get stuck. You've renovated my heart and taken the project all the way! If You start something in my life, I can count on You to follow through on Your word to complete what You've started.

Teach me Your ways, Lord! Show me how to be a good finisher, not just a good starter. Amen.

What would you like God to finish?

I Won't Give Up

And let us not grow weary of doing good, for in
due season we will reap, if we do not give up.
GALATIANS 6:9 ESV

On stressful days, my "want-to" seems to disappear, Lord! Exhaustion rules the day. I throw in the towel, convinced things won't end well. To be honest, on days like that I feel like the whole universe is conspiring against me! Then You step in and turn things around, and I'm reminded that I gave up too soon. If I'll just hold on, You will come through for me every single time.

I have a lot to learn about tenacity, Lord—though I can hardly believe I'm saying that, because I've already been through so much! Give me Your stick-to-it-iveness, I pray. Amen.

How did you jump the hurdle the
last time you felt like giving up?

You Created Me, Lord!

As you do not know the path of the wind, or how the body is formed in a mother's womb, so you cannot understand the work of God, the Maker of all things.

ECCLESIASTES 11:5 NIV

The next time I start to fret over this circumstance or that circumstance, remind me of how I was created in my mother's womb, Lord. You didn't leave out one teensy-tiny detail. You formed me long before Mom knew I was coming!

If You took the time to knit me together with such delicacy, surely I can trust You with the running of my life now. You've been running it all along, after all! So I won't fret. (Hey, I didn't fret when I was tucked away in my mother's womb!) I won't worry about how things are going to turn out. (Did I worry then? No way!) I'll trust You now as I trusted You then—wholly and completely. Amen.

How do you feel knowing that the same God who created you sees what you're going through right now?

Keep the Past in the Past

*This is what the LORD says—he who made a way
through the sea, a path through the mighty waters,
who drew out the chariots and horses, the army
and reinforcements together, and they lay there,
never to rise again, extinguished, snuffed out like
a wick: "Forget the former things; do not dwell
on the past. See, I am doing a new thing!"*

ISAIAH 43:16–19 NIV

"Forget the former things." Oh, how easy that sounds, Lord! But how hard it is to do! I have so many regrets, so many unresolved situations. How do I just leave them there? I need Your help to do so.

You've performed so many miracles—rescuing, saving, delivering Your people. And in every situation You offered the same advice: *"Don't look back."* There must be something to it. The past haunts me at times, but I can't look back or I won't move forward. Today I'll do my best to keep my eyes on today, not yesterday. Amen.

What can you do today to put the past in the past?

Bringing Good Cheer

Anxiety weighs down the heart,
but a kind word cheers it up.
PROVERBS 12:25 NIV

I love kind people, Lord! They usually come along at just the right time with a cheerful word. Just one pat on the back, one positive, affirming word, and my entire situation seems to change. Even if the circumstances don't, my attitude does—and that's half the battle. There is great power in the spoken word.

I want to be that kind of person, Father—one who goes around giving pats on the back and speaking encouraging, uplifting words. Stresses will disappear if the world is flooded with encouragers. Help me as I set out on a path to minister to others in this way, I pray. May I penetrate people's hearts with kindness. Amen.

Who can you cheer up today with a kind word?

You've Overcome the World!

"I have said these things to you, that in me you may have peace. In the world you will have tribulation. But take heart; I have overcome the world."

JOHN 16:33 ESV

*I*n this world, I have had trouble. In this world, I have had heartache. Pain. Confusion. Turmoil. In this world, I've been tempted, tried, and wounded.

But You, Lord? You have overcome the world. I don't have to be stressed when trouble comes. I don't have to give in to fear. There's no reason for me to panic when things don't go my way, because You have overcome all of it. There's no problem I will face that You haven't already overcome. So today I reaffirm my trust in You. I place my hand in the hand of the ultimate Overcomer! Amen.

Jesus said these things specifically so that you would have peace. Can you sense His love for you?

Dead Man Walking

After Jesus said this, he cried out in a loud voice, "Lazarus,
come out!" The dead man came out, his hands and feet
wrapped with pieces of cloth, and a cloth around his face.
JOHN 11:43-44 NCV

*W*hy do I waste time worrying about things, Lord? If You
could raise Lazarus from the dead, if You could lift
sick people off their sickbeds, then why would I think You
wouldn't lift me too?

In so many ways I can relate to the Lazarus story. I've never
been physically dead, but there have been times when I felt
like everything had come to an end for me. When I wondered
if there was hope. But You're a Hope Giver! You roll away
stones. You lift my weary head. You turn situations around.

Today I'm "coming forth"—from my worries, my anxieties,
my fears. I'm coming forth to new life, new hope in You. How
I praise You for new beginnings, Lord! Amen.

Has Jesus ever raised you from the dead?

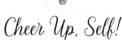

Cheer Up, Self!

When the cares of my heart are many,
your consolations cheer my soul.

PSALM 94:19 ESV

· ·

I remember when I was a kid, Lord, how my schoolteacher
would say, "Turn that frown upside down!" It only takes
a second or two to change a scowl into a smile, and when
the edges of my lips tip up, so does my attitude.

Today I'm asking for a lips-tipped-up sort of day. Even
though my cares are many, You can still cheer my soul. I take
refuge in You, in Your Word, and in Your care. You've got me
covered, so why should I fret?

Cheer up, self! That's my motto of the day. Thanks for
shifting my attitude, Lord! Amen.

· ·

When was the last time you had to cheer
yourself up (spiritually and emotionally)?

I Won't Faint

If you faint in the day of adversity, your strength is small.
PROVERBS 24:10 ESV

Okay, I'll admit it: I give up too easily! Sometimes I "faint in the day of adversity," as Your Word says, Lord. I see a mountain in front of me, and it looms larger than life. Scaling it seems impossible. Instead of speaking to it and expecting it to move, I cower in fear.

Increase my faith today, I pray! I don't want my strength to be small. I want it to be bigger than any mountain and stronger too! I want to be able to look at mountains and speak to them in Jesus' name then watch them tumble into the sea. Thanks for being a Mountain Mover, Lord! Amen.

What are your near-to-fainting triggers?

Rebuilding

*I also told them about the gracious hand of my God
on me and what the king had said to me. They replied,
"Let us start rebuilding." So they began this good work.*

NEHEMIAH 2:18 NIV

Sometimes the tasks in front of me seem too big to take on,
Lord. I get overwhelmed just thinking about all the work
that needs to be done. I get stressed, which only complicates
matters.

Then I'm reminded of the biblical greats, people like
Nehemiah. They faced huge obstacles and encountered
massive challenges, but they forged ahead and saw great
rewards in the end.

When I read about the rebuilding of the wall, I begin
to see things from Your perspective, Lord. You've given me
big tasks, yes, but You've given me all the tools I need to
accomplish what's in front of me to do. I'm so grateful You've
made provision for the big things! Amen.

What has God rebuilt in your life?

The Rock

"He is like a man building a house, who dug deep and laid the foundation on the rock. And when a flood arose, the stream broke against that house and could not shake it, because it had been well built."

LUKE 6:48 ESV

· ·

The wise man built his house upon the rock. I remember singing that song as a child, Lord. Those who are wise choose You as the foundation for their lives.

Nothing has changed from childhood until now. If I want to be successful in any realm of life, then I need to keep my trust in You, not myself. When I hyperfocus on myself, I'm like the man building his house on sand. Everything is bound to crumble.

I'm done with crumbling. I'm done with a self-focused life. From now on, my house will be built on the Rock. Thank You for keeping my spiritual house standing strong, Lord! Amen.

· ·

Is your spiritual house well built?

On Dry Land

Then Moses put out his hand over the sea.
And the Lord moved the sea all night by a
strong east wind. So the waters were divided.
EXODUS 14:21 NLV

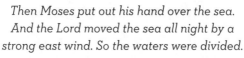

*W*hy do I forget so easily, Lord? It's as if I watch You perform miracle after miracle and then I walk away and forget what You've done. Do I have memory loss? Am I scatterbrained?

I don't want to forget. I want to be reminded every minute of every day that You're more than capable. On top of that, You care! You want the best for me. When I'm facing raging seas, You'll part the waters—not to please Yourself, but so that I can pass over on dry land. I matter to You. My well-being is on Your mind.

I'm going to brush up on the miracles of old so that I have faith for miracles today. Then I'll come to You with a sense of expectation that mountains will move, seas will part, and walking on water really is a possibility. Amen.

When was the last time God intervened in your life in
a miraculous way? Do you believe He'll do it again?

Believing without Seeing

Jesus said to him, "Have you believed because you have seen me? Blessed are those who have not seen and yet have believed."

JOHN 20:29 ESV

"I'll have to see it to believe it." How often have I used those words, Lord? (More than I can count!) I don't want to be a see-it-to-believe-it person any longer. I want to have such strong faith that I can believe something before I see it. I can make my requests with anticipation in my heart that You will come through for me, even when it looks absolutely impossible from all outward appearances.

There's no reason to doubt. You've done it before, and You'll do it again. You're consistent and faithful, even when I'm not. So I'll keep trusting, keep believing, keep hoping, even on the roughest days. Amen.

Are you the "gotta see it to believe it" sort?

A Fruity Response

*But the fruit of the Spirit is love, joy, peace, forbearance,
kindness, goodness, faithfulness, gentleness and
self-control. Against such things there is no law.*
GALATIANS 5:22–23 NIV

When I read this scripture about the fruits of the Spirit, Lord, I wonder if it's possible to have all of them at the very same time. Sometimes I get so stressed out that all of the fruits seem to get tossed from the fruit bowl at once. I lose my joy, I lose my peace, I lose my patience with others, and I'm not kind to anyone.

Stress is a terrible thing! It causes me to say yes when I should say no and to give in to temptation or make wrong decisions. I'm so glad I don't have to live that way! Give me a fruity response, Lord! Amen.

Which fruit is the hardest for you to exhibit?

In Times of Trouble

The LORD is a stronghold for the oppressed,
a stronghold in times of trouble.
PSALM 9:9 ESV

Trouble, trouble. . .everywhere! That's how I feel when I'm going through a stressful season. I turn to the right and bump into trouble. I turn to the left and there it is again. No matter where I go, trouble seems to follow. I often wonder if there's an escape from it or if I'll be plagued by it all my life.

But when I run to You, Lord? No trouble can be found in your courts—only peace, love, forgiveness, and satisfaction. You truly are my stronghold when I'm feeling oppressed. Why would I ever turn to anyone or anything but You? Amen.

Looking back, would you change any
of the troubles you've walked through?

Forget about It!

Now listen, daughter, pay attention, and forget about
your past. Put behind you every attachment to the
familiar, even those who once were close to you!
PSALM 45:10 TPT

*ɣ*ou've asked me to pay attention, Lord, so I'm coming to
You today with eyes wide open. Only when I keep my
focus on You can I truly battle the temptation to look over
my shoulder at the things in my past that still haunt me.

I'm grateful for the reminder that the attachments of
yesterday need to be severed. Today I choose to do that. I
break attachments with toxic relationships, bad attitudes,
poor judgment, and apathy. May my only attachment be to
You, Lord! Amen.

What comes to mind when you read
the words "attachment to the familiar"?

You're My Safe Place

God, you're such a safe and powerful
place to find refuge! You're a proven help
in time of trouble—more than enough and
always available whenever I need you.

PSALM 46:1 TPT

I love this scripture, Lord! There aren't a lot of places to feel safe in this world. I've tried relationships. I've tried money. I've tried climbing the economic ladder. None of those things actually led to long-term safety, though the promises were many.

When I come to You, though? You are truly safe. You are truly powerful. I find refuge in You, my help in time of trouble. Best of all. . .You're always there. I don't have to go searching for You, because You are only a prayer away. How grateful I am! Amen.

How has God been a "proven help" in your times of trouble?

Power from On High

"But you will receive power when the Holy Spirit has come upon you, and you will be my witnesses in Jerusalem and in all Judea and Samaria, and to the end of the earth."

ACTS 1:8 ESV

. . . .

I'll admit it, Lord: I feel like a weakling sometimes. It's as if someone has pulled the plug and zapped me of all my strength, all my energy, all my want-to.

In moments like those, when I'm tempted to give up, I am reminded of the supernatural power that comes from Your Spirit. This holy power invigorates me for the tasks ahead, like letting others know about You and spreading joy to those in need. It also helps me face any challenges that come my way. I'm ready, Lord! Fill me today with Your power. Amen.

. . . .

God can do in a moment what it would take us years to accomplish. How has He proven this in your life?

Harmony

*Live in harmony with one another. Do not
be proud, but be willing to associate with
people of low position. Do not be conceited.*

ROMANS 12:16 NIV

. . . .

*N*ot everyone is easy to get along with, Lord. Of course,
You know this. Some of the people in my world? I would
rather avoid them altogether. They're tough cases, for sure.

Does anyone feel this way about me? I hope not. I don't
want to be known as a contentious, difficult person. I don't
want to be seen as arrogant or prideful. May I be a reflection
of You so that others will be drawn to You when they meet
me. And please show me how to live with (and love) the tough
ones, I pray. Amen.

. . . .

*What can you do today to make a
tough relationship more harmonious?*

You're on My Side, Lord!

*"And that all this assembly may know that the LORD
saves not with sword and spear. For the battle is
the LORD's, and he will give you into our hand."*

1 SAMUEL 17:47 ESV

I'm so grateful for the promise that You are for me, not against me, Lord!

When my enemies dare to raise their heads against me, they are really raising their heads against You! If only they knew that the God of heaven and earth, the all-powerful Author of all, is working on my behalf. Those Goliaths would run the other way if they knew how powerful You are! Prove Yourself today, I pray, so that others will know that You have given the battle into my hand. Amen.

*When did God last prove Himself to your
loved ones by moving on your behalf?*

Those Hard-to-Love People

*"But to you who are listening I say: Love your enemies,
do good to those who hate you, bless those who
curse you, pray for those who mistreat you."*

LUKE 6:27–28 NIV

. . . .

I won't lie, Lord. This verse? It's not my favorite. I would rather *not* love my enemies, thank You very much! This kind of love doesn't come naturally to me. And it certainly doesn't feel natural to do good to those who hate me or, worse yet, mistreat my loved ones.

I'm learning, though. This is the way You want me to live—not just for their benefit but for mine as well. You have a better way. You bless those who bless others. I'm going to give radical love my best shot, but I'll definitely need Your help. Amen.

. . . .

*How can you show love to your
hardest-to-love person today?*

Resting in Him

*Whoever dwells in the shelter of the Most
High will rest in the shadow of the Almighty.*
PSALM 91:1 NIV

I feel like I've stumbled through a lot of dark valleys lately,
Lord. They've cast long, low shadows over me that have
been hard to escape.

But You offer a different kind of shadow. Like a mother
hen extending her wings for her baby chicks to take comfort,
You extend Your arms to me.

Today I come. I come away from the stress. I come away
from the negative feelings. I come away from the chaos. I come
away from those who would seek to hurt me. I come to You
and rest in the shadow of Your wings, Lord. Only there will
I find comfort and peace. Amen.

Are you resting in His shadow today?

I Won't Give In to Fear

*I sought the LORD, and he answered
me and delivered me from all my fears.*

PSALM 34:4 ESV

• •

*I*t's tempting, I'll admit. There are times when I allow myself to give in to fear and doubt. I begin to wallow, much like a pig in his pen. It becomes almost enjoyable to me. Self-pity becomes my best friend. Chaos rules the day.

Then I'm reminded that You never intended for me to live this way! You don't want me to give in to fear. You don't want me to wallow in that hole. You're standing nearby, arms extended, asking me to seek You so that You can deliver me once and for all. So today I seek You with my whole heart and thank You in advance for Your deliverance. Amen.

• •

How can you spend more time seeking Him?

You Keep Your Promises, Lord!

Now the LORD was gracious to Sarah as he had said,
and the LORD did for Sarah what he had promised.
Sarah became pregnant and bore a son to Abraham
in his old age, at the very time God had promised him.

GENESIS 21:1–2 NIV

. . . .

I love the story of Sarah and Abraham, Lord! It's such a wonderful reminder that even the things that feel completely impossible to me are more than possible for You.

If You could cause an elderly woman to conceive and then give birth to a son, then the dreams that You've placed in my heart are more than doable for You! If You could restore Sarah's faith by fulfilling Your promise to her, I know You will do the same in my situation. So I thank you in advance. I will not be found faithless. I won't give in to fear or stress. I put my trust in You and watch You move on my behalf. Amen.

. . . .

What specific promises are you counting on God to keep?

I Need to Let It Go

"For if you forgive others their trespasses,
your heavenly Father will also forgive you,
but if you do not forgive others their trespasses,
neither will your Father forgive your trespasses."
MATTHEW 6:14–15 ESV

I'll be honest. . .I have a hard time letting things go, Lord. I latch on like a dog with a bone sometimes, and then I wonder why I have no peace in my life. The answer is so obvious, but I can't see it. Perhaps I don't want to.

Today's verse is the perfect reminder that there is a way to let go. But it's going to require something of me. If I can loosen my grip. . .if I can learn to forgive people for the things they've done, then You will forgive me. It's a win-win for all of us. I'm going to need Your help, for sure! Intervene in my heart today, I pray. Amen.

Are you holding unforgiveness in
your heart toward anyone today?

A Great Catch

He said, "Throw your net on the right side of the boat and you will find some." When they did, they were unable to haul the net in because of the large number of fish.

JOHN 21:6 NIV

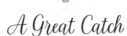

I appreciate how practical You are, God. You always give good advice. To the fishermen You said, *"Throw your net on the right side."* You spoke their language. And because you took the time to do that, they responded.

You speak just as practically to me. You're teaching me how to love those around me by casting a wide net. I want to be loving and patient with people just as You are with me. May I never be found guilty of pushing anyone away from You because of my harsh or bitter outlook. I want to be a true reflection of You in all I say and do. Amen.

Are you standing in the gap for a loved one?

Anxiety, Be Gone!

*So then, banish anxiety from your heart and cast off the
troubles of your body, for youth and vigor are meaningless.*
ECCLESIASTES 11:10 NIV

· ·

Today's verse reminds me of those stories about bad guys
of old being banished to dungeons as a punishment for
their crimes. There, in those deep, dark places, they were
left to ponder their evil ways.

You're asking me to banish anxiety from my heart in
much the same way—to send it to the pit where it belongs. It
has tormented me long enough. The time has come to send
it far, far away. I won't allow it to bog me down any longer.
I have a lot of living to do, after all! So, anxiety, be gone in
Jesus' name! Amen.

· ·

How has the Lord helped you banish anxiety in the past?

Sometimes I Get Angry

*Be angry and do not sin; do not let the sun go down
on your anger, and give no opportunity to the devil.*

EPHESIANS 4:26–27 ESV

I wish I was one of those people who didn't have to struggle with my temper, Lord. But I'll admit. . .there are days when I completely lose it. Stresses take me to the boiling point, and I'm like a teakettle erupting. I can't seem to control myself in those moments.

Your Word says that getting angry is not a sin. But acting on my anger in unhealthy ways? Therein lies the problem. I'm going to need Your help with my temper, for sure. I don't want to hurt those around me by exploding. And I never want the sun to go down on my anger. Give me Your peace to calm the storms inside my heart, I pray. Amen.

How do you calm yourself when your temper flares?

Rivers in the Desert

"Remember not the former things, nor consider the things of old. Behold, I am doing a new thing; now it springs forth, do you not perceive it? I will make a way in the wilderness and rivers in the desert."

ISAIAH 43:18–19 ESV

I have been through parched, dry seasons, Lord. When I look back on my past, I wonder sometimes how I made it through. Then I'm reminded: You made a way every time there seemed to be no way.

You provided rivers in the desert. You gave refreshment when I was weary and dry. You made a path for me to succeed even when it felt impossible. And because You have done this for me in the past, I know You will do it again and again and again. I trust You, Lord. I won't follow any path but Yours. Amen.

When did God last carve a way through the wilderness for you?

I Won't Be Dismayed

*Fear not, for I am with you; be not dismayed, for I
am your God; I will strengthen you, I will help you,
I will uphold you with my righteous right hand.*

ISAIAH 41:10 ESV

*H*eavyhearted. Burdened. Weighed down. Stressed out by
my emotions. These are all phrases that have described
me at one point or another.

I'll confess, I have allowed my emotions to rule me at times.
The heaviness feels like a cross I must bear. But You have
called me to rise above my emotions. You tell me that You will
strengthen me so that I don't have to be afraid or dismayed.

So today I choose Your way. I won't allow my emotions
to dictate how this day plays out. I'm grateful for Your
intervention in my heart and my actions. Amen.

When you're stressed, do you tend to give in to dismay?

Everything I Need

*His divine power has given us everything we
need for a godly life through our knowledge of
him who called us by his own glory and goodness.*

2 PETER 1:3 NIV

Some of the stress in my life comes from not trusting You for my provision, Lord. I'll admit it.

More often than not I get worked up over finances. . . whether there's enough money in the bank to cover the mortgage or adequate groceries in the pantry to feed the family today. You not only provide the tangible things I need, Lord, but also give me all that I need emotionally, spiritually, and psychologically to live a godly life.

Today I look to You for my total provision, inside and out. You've got me covered, so I place my trust in You and choose not to fret. Amen.

What are you asking God for today?

And the Walls Came Tumbling Down!

When the trumpets sounded, the army shouted,
and at the sound of the trumpet, when the men
gave a loud shout, the wall collapsed; so everyone
charged straight in, and they took the city.

JOSHUA 6:20 NIV

They're a safety mechanism, Lord—these walls I've put up. I've fixed them in place so that others can't break through. Unfortunately, I've often built walls between the two of us as well, Lord. I didn't mean for that to happen, but it did. I can sense them in my heart.

Like Joshua when he faced the walls of Jericho, I come to You today in faith, asking for those walls to be torn down once and for all. I want to charge straight into the promised land of Your peace, victorious and fully set free. No matter how long or how far I have to march, those walls will come down in Jesus' name. Amen.

What walls need to come down in your life?

You'll Teach Me All Things

*"But the Helper, the Holy Spirit, whom the Father will
send in my name, he will teach you all things and bring
to your remembrance all that I have said to you."*

JOHN 14:26 ESV

• •

With You, Lord, I feel like I'm getting a college education all over again. I'm on a forever learning curve, but You are teaching me things that no professor could possibly know. You give wisdom and insight and understanding. You offer discernment and peace and joy in place of confusion and frustration.

You are the best teacher around, Lord! Even the things I don't realize I need to know are mine for the taking with You leading the way. I will turn to Your Word, Your way, and Your heart so that I can walk in the fullness of joy You have called me to. Amen.

• •

*Are you still on a learning curve? What
lessons are you struggling to learn?*

Blind Eyes Opened

*Therefore the Pharisees also asked him how he
had received his sight. "He put mud on my eyes,"
the man replied, "and I washed, and now I see."*

JOHN 9:15 NIV

. . . .

I love the story about the blind man receiving his sight. In some ways I feel like I have walked a mile in his shoes. Too many times the enemy has blinded me to Your love, Your compassion, Your direction. He's tricky!

But those blinders have fallen off now! You've given me supernatural 20/20 vision so that I can see things the way You see them, respond to others as You would respond to them. When I'm using this vision, it puts my stresses in perspective. I see them as what they really are—stepping-stones to something better.

Thank You for making blind eyes see, Lord. Amen.

. . . .

*Has God ever given you supernatural
sight to see things as He does?*

Every Hidden Thing

*Fear God and keep his commandments, for this
is the duty of all mankind. For God will bring
every deed into judgment, including every
hidden thing, whether it is good or evil.*

ECCLESIASTES 12:13–14 NIV

They think they can get away with it, Lord. Those things they do in secret? They're sure You won't notice. The way they've hurt me. The way they've wounded my loved ones. They think their actions are fine and good, that there will be no price to pay.

But You are exacting a price even now. You're drawing evil deeds out of the darkness and into the light. Today I pray for deliverance from my enemies, the very ones who hurt me. As You deal with them, may I learn to forgive so that I can be set free—and ultimately so that they can be set free as well. Thank You, Lord. Amen.

When did God last deliver you from your enemies?

I Won't Wear My Shame

*Instead of your shame there shall be a double
portion; instead of dishonor they shall rejoice in
their lot; therefore in their land they shall possess
a double portion; they shall have everlasting joy.*

ISAIAH 61:7 ESV

Some of the people I know wear their shame on their
sleeves, Lord. I can sense it, feel it when I'm around them.

I don't want to be like that. You've taken my shame.
You've taken my past. There's no reason to let my yesterdays
add any stress to my todays. In place of shame, You've given
me a happy heart. You've blessed me with everlasting joy in
place of sorrow over past indiscretions.

I love the way Your plan works, Lord. You swap out my
bad for Your good. I will never understand such love, but I'm
grateful all the same. Amen.

How can you let go of stress-inducing shame today?

Stressing Over a Friend in Need

Some men took a man who was not able to move his body to Jesus. He was carried on a bed. They looked for a way to take the man into the house where Jesus was. But they could not find a way to take him in because of so many people. They made a hole in the roof over where Jesus stood. Then they let the bed with the sick man on it down before Jesus.

LUKE 5:18–19 NLV

You know who she is, Lord. You know how much I care about her, how worried I've been about her. You know how many sleepless nights I've spent wondering if she will make it through this. Her situation seems too far gone, and I'm fretting over it.

Today I ask that You take charge, not just of her circumstances but of my heart and any role I play in this. I give this situation and this loved one to You, once and for all. Amen.

How do you decide when to help a friend. . .and when not to?

I'm Not Helpless

Strengthen the feeble hands, steady the knees that give
way; say to those with fearful hearts, "Be strong, do not
fear; your God will come, he will come with vengeance;
with divine retribution he will come to save you."

ISAIAH 35:3–4 NIV

Okay, I'll admit it, Lord: sometimes I act like I'm totally helpless. I allow myself to give in to defeat and despair instead of reminding myself that I have the best Helper ever ready to come out swinging on my behalf.

You are the best, after all! You helped David take down Goliath. You helped Joshua take down the walls of Jericho. You remind me through Your Word that I can cross the sea on dry land.

Why would I ever doubt Your ability or Your love for Your children, Lord? Thank You, my Lord and Helper. I lean on You today. Amen.

How can you remind yourself today that God really will
come to save you, that He won't leave you utterly helpless?

You Rejoice over Me

*"The LORD your God is with you, the Mighty
Warrior who saves. He will take great delight
in you; in his love he will no longer rebuke
you, but will rejoice over you with singing."*

ZEPHANIAH 3:17 NIV

Oh, how I love the image this verse presents! I'm down here on Planet Earth, feeling stressed out and worried. And what are You up to, Lord? With joy, You are singing and dancing over me. You haven't got a care in the world! (Or the universe, as the case may be.)

You haven't given up on my situation. You're already in celebration mode. That perspective changes everything. Today, may I rejoice—may I praise and sing and celebrate—even before I see the victory. Give me Your heavenly perspective, I pray. Amen.

*Does it thrill your heart to know
that God is singing over you?*

I Won't Doubt

*But when you ask, you must believe and not
doubt, because the one who doubts is like a
wave of the sea, blown and tossed by the wind.*

JAMES 1:6 NIV

* * *

*W*hen I come to You, Lord, I must confess that I don't always have sufficient faith to believe You're actually going to do what I'm asking you to do. My requests are huge at times, but my faith is very small.

I don't want to be like a wave blown and tossed by the wind. I want to be firm, steady, like a rock. Today, please take my doubts. Take my fears. Take away that nagging feeling that things are going to get worse instead of better. Replace those feelings with confidence, not in myself but in You. Amen.

* * *

What can you do to remain steady when the winds blow?

Patience Is a Virtue

*Love is patient, love is kind. It does not envy,
it does not boast, it is not proud. It does not
dishonor others, it is not self-seeking, it is not
easily angered, it keeps no record of wrongs.*

1 CORINTHIANS 13:4–5 NIV

. . . .

*L*ove is patient. I could stop right there while reading this verse because I know that I'm not always the most patient person around, which must mean I'm not showing adequate love at times, Lord. This has been a shortcoming in my life, I admit.

You've been so patient with me, heavenly Father! So many times You could have scolded or rebuked, but instead You chose to love me through the situation, in spite of my mistakes. Now it's time for me to start showing that same kind of patience to others, even those who stumble and fall more than their fair share. Show me how to exhibit patience to the difficult ones, I pray. Amen.

. . . .

*Love is patient. Do you exhibit God's
patience in showing love to others?*

You Go Above and Beyond!

*They all ate and were satisfied, and the disciples picked
up twelve basketfuls of broken pieces that were left over.*
MATTHEW 14:20 NIV

*A*verage has never been good enough for You, Lord! You
created giraffes with elevator-length necks. You created
flamingos with long, skinny legs. You created mountain peaks
so high we can't possibly climb them.

You're an "above and beyond" sort of God. And because
You've always been willing to go above and beyond with Your
children, I want to learn to do the same for others. That same
generosity, that same exuberance to do more. . .may it be
mine as well. May no one ever accuse me of being normal
or average! Amen.

*When was the last time God surprised
you by going above and beyond?*

Called to Be a Disciple

*When Jesus had called the Twelve together, he gave
them power and authority to drive out all demons
and to cure diseases, and he sent them out to
proclaim the kingdom of God and to heal the sick.*
LUKE 9:1-2 NIV

I'll admit it, Lord: I'm not always the best at playing along
in a group setting. Sometimes I like to be the one in
charge. I enjoy dishing out instructions, but I'm not so keen
on taking them.

Being Your disciple, however? I am more than happy to
submit to Your authority, God! You offer me something that
no other leader does—power to pray with faith, to believe for
miracles. Authority to overcome even the biggest adversities.
Best of all, You give me joy for the journey. I can always
trust in You. Being Your disciple is a privilege, an honor, a
challenge, and a joy! Amen.

*God has given you authority just as He gave the first
disciples authority. When was the last time you used it?*

You Come Through for Your Own

*"My God sent his angel, and he shut the mouths
of the lions. They have not hurt me, because I
was found innocent in his sight. Nor have I ever
done any wrong before you, Your Majesty."*

DANIEL 6:22 NIV

Daniel in the lions' den. The three Hebrew men in the
fiery furnace. David facing down the giant. Your Word
is filled with stories of people who faced great trials and
seemingly impossible situations.

Time and again You've come through for Your own! You
delivered Daniel from the mouths of the lions. He wasn't
harmed at all by those ferocious beasts. What a miracle!
So why do I fret? Why do I forget that the same God who
delivered Daniel stands ready to deliver me?

Thank You, my miracle-working God. Amen.

Has God shut the mouths of lions for you?

I'm Bringing It to You, Lord

*"This, then, is how you should pray:
'Our Father in heaven, hallowed be your name.'"*
MATTHEW 6:9 NIV

. . . .

H ow many times have I run to others with my problems,
Lord? Too many to count! I go to friends. I go to loved
ones. I whine and complain to my best friend or take my
gripes to social media for the masses to share.

Sometimes You're the last one on my list. I wonder why
I'm so stressed out, and then I realize I haven't connected
with the only One who can actually transform the situation
for me. So, Lord, I come to You today. I bring my grievances
and my woes to You, along with my joys and celebrations.

May I never forget to come to You first. Amen.

. . . .

*Have you ever run to friends or an
addiction instead of going to Jesus?*

Friends Who Have My Back

Then Jonathan made a covenant with David,
because he loved him as his own soul.
1 SAMUEL 18:3 ESV

I love the story of David and Jonathan, Lord! It's so wonderful to have a bosom friend, someone you can confide in. She not only keeps your secrets but also prays for you, encourages you, and is always there when you need her.

I long to be that kind of friend to others, one who is trustworthy and true. Speaking of amazing friends, You are the best, Jesus! When I can trust no other, I can put my faith in You. When others let me down, I know You never will. You are the best friend I could ever have, and I'm overwhelmed with gratitude! Amen.

Which friends do you "love as your own soul"?

Your Promises Are Sure

*"I am putting my rainbow in the clouds as the sign
of the agreement between me and the earth."*
GENESIS 9:13 NCV

....

*Y*ou hung a rainbow in the sky to remind Noah of Your
promise that You would never again flood the earth,
Lord. All I have to do is look up on a rainy day and see those
brilliant colors shimmering overhead to be reminded that
You always keep Your word. If You say it, You will do it. Your
promises are sure.

My promises? Not so much. I often fall short of doing
what I say I will do. I need reminding. You, Lord? I never
have to remind You. You provide, and at just the right time.
How grateful I am for the assurance of Your promises. Amen.

....

Are you the kind of person who needs and likes reminders?

I'm Building My House on the Rock

"Everyone then who hears these words of mine and does them will be like a wise man who built his house on the rock. And the rain fell, and the floods came, and the winds blew and beat on that house, but it did not fall, because it had been founded on the rock."

MATTHEW 7:24–25 ESV

. . . .

The wise man built his house upon the rock, and the rains came tumbling down. I remember the lesson of that little song! If I build my life on You, Jesus, the rains can come tumbling down, but I will stand strong. If I build my life on material things, I can expect emotional upheaval and chaos.

Sounds like a pretty easy choice to me, Lord. I will build my house on You and stand strong even when the stresses of life come in like a flood. Thanks for being my Rock. Amen.

. . . .

Is your spiritual house built on the Rock?

I'm Putting You First

"But seek first the kingdom of God and his righteousness, and all these things will be added to you."

Matthew 6:33 esv

. . . .

I need to keep You in Your rightful place, Lord! I don't always do that, I confess. Many times I put my own wants and wishes, my own hopes and dreams, above my passion for You. Sometimes I even put the wants and wishes of others above the things You have clearly called me to do.

I'm so sorry for all of the times I didn't put You first. You are Lord of all and deserving of Your rightful place in my heart and my life. When I put things in the proper order, the storms quiet, the seas grow still, and my heart is at peace. How I praise You for the peace You bring! Amen.

. . . .

What does it mean to put God first?

You're a God Who Supplies

"For this is what the LORD, the God of Israel, says: 'The jar of flour will not be used up and the jug of oil will not run dry until the day the LORD sends rain on the land.'"
1 KINGS 17:14 NIV

Oh, how I love the stories of Your provision! You fed the multitude with five loaves of bread and two fish. You fed the prophet Elijah with a near-empty jar of flour and oil. You made sure the Israelites had manna and quail in the desert.

You always provide. In fact, You go above and beyond. So why would I doubt that You would do the same for me?

Today, I will trust You for my provision—the needs in my bank account, my pantry, even my heart. You're going to pour out blessings on me above what I could ask or think, Lord, and I'm ready with hands extended! Amen.

Has the Lord ever provided for you in a supernatural way?

I'm Learning from Your Creation

"But ask the beasts, and they will teach you; the birds of the heavens, and they will tell you; or the bushes of the earth, and they will teach you; and the fish of the sea will declare to you. Who among all these does not know that the hand of the LORD has done this? In his hand is the life of every living thing and the breath of all mankind."

JOB 12:7–10 ESV

Caterpillars that morph into butterflies. Ocean waves that pound against the shore and then return to the sea to begin the process all over again. Mountain peaks that stand jagged and strong. I marvel at Your creation, Lord! These things delight me for they all point to You. Even the harshest things, like storm winds or fierce animals, are a reminder of Your grandeur.

You didn't miss a thing when You created the universe, Lord. So why would I ever think You would overlook the details of my life? You know. . .and You care. If You cared enough to make a giraffe's neck long enough to nibble from the trees above, surely You can take care of me. Amen.

What's your favorite part of God's creation?

Your Face Shines upon Me

"The LORD bless you and keep you; the LORD make his face shine on you and be gracious to you; the LORD turn his face toward you and give you peace."
NUMBERS 6:24–26 NIV

I'll admit it, Lord. There are seasons when I feel overlooked. Forgotten. I wonder if the people in my world even remember I'm here at all. The stresses of my everyday life add up, but no one is around to share the load. No one seems to have time.

Then I remember this verse, and I can't help but smile. You're blessing me even during the stressful seasons. You're keeping me in good times and bad. You're making Your face shine upon me.

Wow! I could pause right there and lift my hands in celebration! The radiant blessing of Your holy presence brings peace to my soul, Lord. Thank You for shining down on me. Amen.

How do you sense God's face shining upon you?

Hope for the Future

There is surely a future hope for you,
and your hope will not be cut off.
PROVERBS 23:18 NIV

Sometimes I'm fickle. I lose hope so quickly. I forget the marvelous blessings of yesterday (or even five minutes ago) and give up before the battle has even begun.

You're not a "giving up" sort of God. No, You're always reminding me that there's hope, no matter how bleak things look. And You're not keen on letting me give up either, are You, Lord? You nudge me to keep going even when my feelings dictate otherwise.

There is surely a future hope for me. So I really don't have anything to worry about, do I? If it's sure, if it's certain. . .then I have nothing to fear. Today, I lay down my worries and ask for faith to believe that my tomorrows are already in Your hands. Amen.

How does the word "surely" drive
home the point of today's verse?

You've Given Your Angels Instructions!

*For he will command his angels concerning
you to guard you in all your ways.*

PSALM 91:11 NIV

D o You have daily meetings with Your angels, Lord? I often wonder about this. Are specific angels assigned to me? If so, I surely keep them very busy. You're probably having to give them instructions around the clock. They probably hear the words *"Keep a special eye on this one!"* a lot.

I rest easy in the knowledge that You have a plan for my protection, Lord. You've commanded Your angels to guard me, not just during good seasons but during the hard times as well. Your Word assures me that they're watching over me "in all [my] ways." When I make mistakes. When I do well. When I'm stressed. When I'm walking in peace. They're right there, watching over me. Thank You for caring so much, Lord. I take comfort in Your care. Amen.

Are your angels working overtime?

I Want What I Want

Incline my heart to your testimonies, and not to selfish gain!
PSALM 119:36 ESV

Sometimes my stress is caused by not getting my way, Lord. I want what I want, and I want it now. It's hard for me to acknowledge that not getting my way often leads to pity parties or anxiety, but that's the truth.

You never meant for Your kids to be selfish, did You? You long for us to keep our eyes riveted on You, not ourselves. Your heart's desire is for us to love others as we love ourselves. Selfish gain was never part of Your plan for any of us.

Help me with this, I pray. I don't want to get worked up over every little thing that doesn't go my way. Instead, I want to remain true to Your calling—to love You first with a deep and abiding passion, to love others sincerely, and to love myself as You love me. Help me, I pray. Amen.

How can you trade your way for God's way?

Authenticity

For our boast is this, the testimony of our conscience,
that we behaved in the world with simplicity and
godly sincerity, not by earthly wisdom but by the
grace of God, and supremely so toward you.

2 CORINTHIANS 1:12 ESV

I've seen phony-baloney people, Lord. Many are over-the-top, an exaggerated version of themselves. I wonder how others can fall for their nonsense.

You long for me to be authentic even if it means I'm not the most popular person out there. "Fitting in" isn't as important as pleasing Your heart, so I'll do my best to be who You created me to be—nothing more and nothing less. Sincerity is far more important to You than anything else. You're not keen on fakes.

May I live with authenticity, use my gifts with a genuine desire to serve others, and worship You with a sincere heart. May there be no pretense in me, I pray. Amen.

Does God want you to fake it until you make it?

Great and Unsearchable Things

*"Call to me and I will answer you and tell you great
and unsearchable things you do not know."*

JEREMIAH 33:3 NIV

You will show me great and unsearchable things, Lord. Things my finite mind could never begin to comprehend. Things so far beyond me that people will stand in awe. You have wisdom, Lord, that can't be found in books or university classrooms. The kind of knowledge I gain from You comes from on high, not gleaned from humans but imparted straight from the heart of the Creator of all.

You have asked me to call on You. When I do, You answer. But You don't just give a short, quick answer. No, You begin to pour out Your heart, revealing great and unsearchable things that, until that very moment, were completely unknown to me. What a gift! What a blessing! Oh, to hear from You daily! Amen.

*Have you ever received unsearchable
knowledge straight from the heart of God?*

I'm on a Learning Curve

Now when Jesus saw the crowds, he went up on a mountainside and sat down. His disciples came to him, and he began to teach them.

MATTHEW 5:1-2 NIV

Some days I feel like a student in a classroom. The learning curve is steep, Lord! Just about the time I think I've got things figured out, I realize there are areas of my life where I need a tutorial. Thank goodness You're the best Tutor around! You're gentle, patient, and loving in the way You share your wisdom and knowledge with me.

Today I open my heart, my mind, and my imagination so that I can learn all that You have for me today. Even the circumstances that are stressing me out or causing pain can be teaching tools in Your hands, Father. Have Your way in me today, I pray. Amen.

Are you on a learning curve at the moment?

Protector and Defender

What then shall we say to these things?
If God is for us, who can be against us?
ROMANS 8:31 ESV

$\mathcal{Y}$ ou are for me. Those four words change absolutely everything, Lord. When I'm facing trials. When I come up against a health crisis. When I'm battling manipulation or narcissism. You are for me. You are not against me. You want me to succeed.

My enemies stand no chance, no matter how hard they fight. No matter how tricky their schemes. No matter how sly their approach. You see all, hear all, and intervene in all. What You have ordained cannot be stopped. Thank You, God, for serving as my Protector and Defender, the One who is always on my side. Amen.

Do you believe that God is bigger than your problems?

I Give Up, Lord!

From inside the fish Jonah prayed to the LORD his God. He said: "In my distress I called to the LORD, and he answered me. From deep in the realm of the dead I called for help, and you listened to my cry."

JONAH 2:1–2 NIV

• •

I'm tired of running, Lord! I give up. You've been chasing me down for a long time. And now You've caught up with me, finding me in a deep place, a trap of my own choosing. Like Jonah, I'm stuck. . .stressed, worried, defeated.

You have me right where You want me. You finally have my undivided attention, Lord! I'm all Yours. What else can I do but listen? What else can I do but ponder Your way instead of my own? I cry out to You today from the belly of the whale. Thank You, God, that even here You hear my cry and respond in love. Amen.

• •

Has God ever placed you in the proverbial belly of a whale?

More Time with You, Lord!

*Draw near to God, and he will draw near
to you. Cleanse your hands, you sinners,
and purify your hearts, you double-minded.*

JAMES 4:8 ESV

My life tends to be a little crazy, Lord. I feel like I'm always rushing here or there, shuttling the kids to T-ball practice or gymnastics, taking someone to the doctor, dealing with work-related challenges. Chaos abounds most days, and there's no time left over to draw near to You. Or so I claim.

Quiet time with You has been the missing ingredient in my life. Do I wonder why things are stressful? I haven't invited You in. Today I step away from the chaos long enough to say, "Lord, here I am." You have my full attention. I am Yours, not just for a few moments but for all eternity. Nothing is more important than spending time with You. May I never forget it. Amen.

What does it mean to draw near to God?

Greater Things Ahead!

For I consider that the sufferings of this present time are not worth comparing with the glory that is to be revealed to us.

ROMANS 8:18 ESV

Sometimes I look at the sufferings going on around me, and I get overwhelmed. So much drama is going on in the world today, Lord. So much sickness. So much division and anger. I wonder how long humanity can go on like this.

When I see things through Your lens, I'm reminded that these current sufferings, whether they are my own or ones affecting my loved ones, can't begin to compare with the glory that is coming. The contrast of chaos to glory is going to be breathtaking. So please guard us during these tumultuous times. Prepare our hearts for greater things ahead. Amen.

When you look through the lens of eternity, is your current situation more tolerable?

You'll Work It Out

And we know that for those who love God
all things work together for good, for those
who are called according to his purpose.

ROMANS 8:28 ESV

$\mathcal{Y}$ ou haven't called me to excel so that eyes can be drawn to me, Lord. The purpose behind my successes is to draw humankind to You. That's why You are working all things out—not so that I can be glorified for my achievements but so that others will see You for who You are.

You promise to work things out. That's enough for me. Confusion, misunderstandings, frustrations. . .they are not too big for You. In fact, they are springboards to something better ahead. I can't wait to see what You're going to do, Lord—how You're going to turn my messes into messages for a lost world. Amen.

Are you called according to God's purpose?

You're Straightening My Path

*Trust in the LORD with all your heart and lean not
on your own understanding; in all your ways submit
to him, and he will make your paths straight.*
PROVERBS 3:5–6 NIV

Oh boy, have I ever had some crooked paths over the years! I feel like I've been lost in the wilderness more times than I can count. From the mountains to the valleys, I've trekked a mile or two. . .and often in the wrong direction.

Today I will be the first to admit that my internal compass isn't always the best. Sometimes I set off on my way only to discover it's the wrong way. Thank You for stopping me in my tracks. Thank You for caring enough to straighten the road before me. I'm so grateful for Your intervention in seasons like these. You are my Guardian, my Protector, my true Compass. How I praise You for Your perfect direction. Amen.

*When was the last time you realized
God was straightening your path?*

A Cloud of Witnesses

Therefore, since we are surrounded by so great a cloud of witnesses, let us also lay aside every weight, and sin which clings so closely, and let us run with endurance the race that is set before us.

HEBREWS 12:1 ESV

. . . .

Whenever I feel alone, Lord, I reflect on the biblical giants from years past. Men like Abraham, Isaac, and Jacob. Women like Sarah, Deborah, and Mary. Warriors like Gideon, David, and Jehoshaphat.

I can picture them all in the grandstands watching me run my race. They're waving banners and cheering me on. I can hear them shouting, "You've got this!" I can hear Mary crying out, "Keep the faith! Don't give up!" Their voices ring loud in my ears as I continue to run. Thank You for the stories of the saints of old, Lord. They inspire me to keep going. Amen.

. . . .

Who do you imagine is cheering in the grandstands, giving you the courage to keep going?

Steadfast under Trial

Blessed is the man who remains steadfast under trial,
for when he has stood the test he will receive the crown
of life, which God has promised to those who love him.
JAMES 1:12 ESV

I will stand the test. Maybe I should embroider that on a sampler and hang it on the wall. To be reminded daily would encourage me so much.

You have a lovely prize waiting on the other end of my steadfastness, Lord. I'll spend eternity with You, where the testing will be behind me. The victory came not by my own actions but by Your sacrifice on the cross, Jesus. And I get to share in the prize—eternal bliss with You.

Thank You for helping me stand during the various tests I go through. I've got this with You leading the way. Amen.

What does it mean to stand the test?

Out of My Distress

Out of my distress I called on the LORD; the LORD answered me and set me free. The LORD is on my side; I will not fear. What can man do to me?

PSALM 118:5-6 ESV

. . . .

*A*s a parent, I know what it's like for my child to come to me when he's in distress. I want him to come to me with everything, but I'm especially attuned to his pleas when he's hurting or in turmoil. I wonder if that's how You feel when I cry out to You in my distress, Lord.

Your heart is touched, I know, because I've seen Your swift and loving responses to those cries. You're on my side, so I have nothing to be afraid of. That reality brings me great comfort no matter what I'm facing. And knowing I have someone to turn to, especially when everything and everyone seems to be against me? Priceless.

Thank You, Lord, for hearing my cries. Amen.

. . . .

When you're in distress, who do you call on?

Table Food

Anyone who lives on milk cannot understand the teaching about being right with God. He is a baby.
HEBREWS 5:13 NLV

$\mathcal{I}$'ve enjoyed my baby food for years now, Lord. I'm comfortable hearing sermons about love, joy, and happiness. Easy messages like "Three Steps to a Better Life" get my vote every time. It's tougher to hear messages about pain, valleys, and sacrifice. Those things require work on my part.

You're calling me to bigger, better things. I can only get there if I'm willing to go deep with You. So today I'll start digging—past the chaos, past the confusion, past the point where I'm comfortable. I'll keep going until I reach that place of revelation where Your truth plants itself deep in my heart. No more milk for me, Lord. I want to fully understand what it means to walk in fullness of peace with You. Amen.

Are you interested in knowing more about the deep things of God?

Called by Kindness

In his kindness God called you to share in his eternal glory by means of Christ Jesus. So after you have suffered a little while, he will restore, support, and strengthen you, and he will place you on a firm foundation.

1 PETER 5:10 NLT

*Y*our kindness, Lord, is what leads me to repentance. I would still be moving in the wrong direction, headed down a dark path, if not for Your gentle and loving ways.

You love me so completely that You would go to great lengths to win my heart. Your kindness draws me to You, and in Your presence I find restoration. I find support. I garner the strength to keep moving ahead.

Best of all, Lord, You've placed my feet on solid rock. Everything in my life is made new because of Your great kindness. How grateful I am! Amen.

How have you personally witnessed the kindness of God in a recent situation?

Let Anxieties Go

And he said to his disciples, "Therefore I tell you,
do not be anxious about your life, what you will
eat, nor about your body, what you will put on."
LUKE 12:22 ESV

You've told me, *"Don't worry about it!"* But I still fret, Lord. I wonder how the light bill will get paid this month. Should I juggle the other bills around so I can pay that one? I'm also worked up about a situation at work. My coworkers aren't getting along, and the tension is grating on my nerves, making my job more difficult.

In moments like these, when I'm stressed out, You say, *"Don't be anxious about your life—what you eat, put on, and so forth."* I need Your help to refrain from worry, though. It's not coming naturally to me. Help me to let go of the anxieties I'm clinging so tightly to today, Father! I need Your help to unwind my fingers from them! Amen.

How do you keep from fretting
when you're in a season of lack?

Your Spirit Is There

*In the beginning God created the heavens and
the earth. Now the earth was formless and empty,
darkness was over the surface of the deep, and the
Spirit of God was hovering over the waters.*

GENESIS 1:1-2 NIV

. . . .

*Y*our Spirit hovered over the waters at creation. How miraculous that must have been—how powerful! Your Spirit changes everything!

I read this verse and realize Your Spirit is hovering over me right now, in this very moment, even as I read these words. Your Spirit is here to comfort, to lead, to guide. To give power. To stir me to action.

I have nothing to fear, no matter what I face. Your Spirit is with me. How grateful I am! Amen.

. . . .

*Can you think of a particular time when
you deeply sensed God's presence?*

Joy in Place of Sorrow

*"So also you have sorrow now, but I will
see you again, and your hearts will rejoice,
and no one will take your joy from you."*
JOHN 16:22 ESV

*Y*ou're not content for me to live in sorrow, Lord. No way!
You have a plan to replace it with joy. The thought of
being able to rejoice again seems impossible when sorrows
are fresh, but hindsight is 20/20. You've refreshed my spirit
so many times in my life, and I know You will do it again.

Joy is birthed out of hope, so today I place my hope in
You. I won't let circumstances dictate how I move forward.
I'll press onward with Your hand in mine. I'll allow joy to lead
the way, even when troubles come. I won't let my struggles
zap me of my joy. It's Your gift to me, after all! I'll hold on
tight, for in You I find my strength. Amen.

Has God ever changed your sorrow to joy in an instant?

Eyes Wide Open

Be alert and of sober mind. Your enemy the devil prowls
around like a roaring lion looking for someone to devour.
1 PETER 5:8 NIV

*Y*ou tell me to be alert, Lord. Yet half the time I forget to keep my eyes open, and then I wonder how the enemy sneaks in to catch me off guard. If I'm really staying alert, if I'm not allowing emotions and turmoil to cloud my mind, then I'll see his tactics. Problem is, I'm often worked up about something or frustrated with someone, and the enemy uses my angst as the perfect opportunity to waltz into the room.

I won't let him prowl today, Lord. My eyes are wide open. I'm on to him. When that roaring lion comes around, I'll take him down in Jesus' name. Amen.

What happens when you're not paying attention?

You're Close When My Heart Is Broken

The LORD is close to the brokenhearted;
he rescues those whose spirits are crushed.

PSALM 34:18 NLT

You're always nearby, Lord, but I feel especially comforted knowing You're there when my heart is broken. Usually when I reach that point, I feel completely isolated, all alone. But You've made a point of telling me that You're there even then.

Best of all, You're there with a plan to rescue me. You long to scoop my crushed spirit into Your tender hands and gently breathe life into it again. So I give You the broken pieces inside of me, Lord. I say, "Come and do what only You can do." Mend. Repair. Heal. Restore. Draw close and do a deep work, I pray. Amen.

Can you think of a time when
God healed your broken heart?

Praising in the Stressful Seasons

Rejoice always, pray continually, give thanks in all circumstances; for this is God's will for you in Christ Jesus.
1 THESSALONIANS 5:16–18 NIV

My head hurts, Lord. My stomach is churning. I feel like I'm tied up in knots! The very last thing I feel like doing right now is praising You. But Your Word says I should praise even in these stressful circumstances. When I'm off my game. When everything is against me. Right here. Right now. Without hesitation.

To be honest, I'd rather pull the covers over my head. But I'll try it Your way, Father! I lift Your name right now, Lord, and I say, "Thank You for being such a good and loving Father! Thank You for Your provision. Thank You for answers to my many questions. Thank You for bringing calm in the middle of the storm."

Aah, that's better! One moment of praise changes everything! Amen.

Are you in a stressful season? If so, why not lift your eyes to heaven and begin to praise Him!

I Won't Lean on My Own Understanding

Trust in the LORD with all your heart,
and do not lean on your own understanding.

PROVERBS 3:5 ESV

I'm one of those people who thinks I have to figure everything out on my own, Lord. I work things out in my head and then rework them to come up with a better plan, one that will surely succeed. Many times I've moved forward, confident with my decision, only to find out it was the wrong one.

You ask me to place my confidence in You, not myself. You want me to lean on Your understanding, not my own. Show me how to do that, I pray. Lead me in Your ways that I might be more effective for You. Amen.

Where does your own understanding lead you?

My Spirit Is Willing, Lord

*"Watch and pray so that you will not fall into temptation.
The spirit is willing, but the flesh is weak."*

MATTHEW 26:41 NIV

How many times have I used the words "I'll do that tomorrow"? My desire is strong as long as I don't have to step out in faith immediately. But when it comes time to actually take that first step? Too often my flesh is weak. I can't seem to get myself going. The energy just isn't there.

I especially need Your help on those days, Lord! You can energize me with Your Spirit and give me all I need to take that first step! I thank You in advance for strengthening this physical body. Amen.

*How do you move forward on days when
your spirit is willing but your flesh is weak?*

Escape Hatch

The only temptation that has come to you is that which everyone has. But you can trust God, who will not permit you to be tempted more than you can stand. But when you are tempted, he will also give you a way to escape so that you will be able to stand it.

1 CORINTHIANS 10:13 NCV

*Y*ou don't want me to get caught in the enemy's traps, Lord. That's why, with every tempting situation that comes along, You provide an escape. You make provision in advance, knowing I'll need it!

I don't always see the way out, so today I'm asking for Your supernatural vision so that I can see what You see. Show me the escape hatch, and then give me the guidance I need to take it! I'm so grateful for a way out of life's temptations. Amen.

Can you think of a particular time when God provided a supernatural escape hatch to get you out of a tempting situation?

You're Sending Help!

Two are better than one, because they have a
good return for their labor: If either of them falls
down, one can help the other up. But pity anyone
who falls and has no one to help them up.

ECCLESIASTES 4:9-10 NIV

You never meant for us to do life alone, Lord. It was always Your plan that we would lean on each other, learn from each other, and benefit from each other.

Many times, especially during stressful seasons, I pull away from the people in my circle. I don't want to burden them. But through this verse You are reminding me that two really are better than one. My plan for getting out of life's messes needs to involve leaning on the ones You've given me to love. Thank You for this reminder. Amen.

Who do you want by your side during the tough seasons?

Every Good Work

*And God is able to bless you abundantly, so
that in all things at all times, having all that you
need, you will abound in every good work.*

2 CORINTHIANS 9:8 NIV

. . . .

In all things at all times, you want me to abound in good
works, Lord!

All things. Every venture. Every relationship. Every
financial decision. Every academic endeavor. You want me
to be blessed abundantly. *All* is a lot!

I'm preparing my heart even now for Your blessing. I
feel such great joy knowing that You passionately want to
provide for me so that I can thrive in every situation. How I
praise You for Your loving care! May I be found worthy of it
as I work for You, Lord. Amen.

. . . .

What does it mean to "abound" in every good work?

You've Got This

*"For I know the plans I have for you," says the
LORD. "They are plans for good and not for
disaster, to give you a future and a hope."*
JEREMIAH 29:11 NLT

• •

*Y*ou know the plans You have for me, Lord. In fact, You
know them well because You are the One who came
up with them in the first place.

I'll confess, there are times I wish I could know them too.
The "not knowing" is difficult at times. But I take comfort in
the fact that You not only know what's coming but are working
out the details even now. In this very moment, you are putting together plans for my tomorrows. How wonderful to
know that You are already there, and what a privilege to be
able to step into those plans with Your hand in mine! Thank
You, heavenly Father. Amen.

• •

Are your current plans His or yours?

As a Mother Comforts Her Child

"I will comfort you there in Jerusalem
as a mother comforts her child."
ISAIAH 66:13 NLT

*N*o one comforts like a mother does. Her heart is intrinsically tied to her children. She feels their pain. She senses their frustrations. She knows their cries, their needs, and she's right there, ready to step in at a moment's notice.

You are like that tender mother, Lord! You know Your children so well. You know when I sit and when I rise. You know when my heart is broken and when I'm feeling strong. And You are right there, ready to comfort, to touch, and to wipe away every tear. What a tender Father You are. I am Your grateful child. Amen.

How has God comforted you in the past?
How is He comforting you even now?

Keeping My Cool

*Do not be quickly provoked in your spirit,
for anger resides in the lap of fools.*

ECCLESIASTES 7:9 NIV

• •

I've been in some situations where I erupted quickly,
like a volcano that offered no warning. I'm sure my swift
reaction startled others in the room! I was a little startled
myself. Talk about a lava flow.

You ask me *not* to erupt, Lord. Today's verse reminds me
that it's not good to be quickly provoked in my spirit. Only
fools blow up like that! Oops! Calm my heart in the moment,
I pray. The next time I'm tempted to blow my top, stop me in
my tracks and bring peace to my soul. Intervene, I pray. Amen.

• •

*What techniques do you use when
you're about to lose your cool?*

Armed and Ready

You have armed me with strength for the battle;
you have subdued my enemies under my feet.

PSALM 18:39 NLT

You saw this battle coming, didn't You, Lord? You knew the enemies I would face. You knew the struggles in my heart. You saw it all long before it happened.

Best of all, You've already made provision for this battle. You have armed me. You have made me strong. All along You've been prepping me for this moment. With Your hand in mine, I will take down the enemy of my soul. I will let him know that the God of creation is on my side! How I praise You for joining me in the battle. Amen.

Do you feel armed and ready right now?

Mustard Seed Faith

"You don't have enough faith," Jesus told them. "I tell you the truth, if you had faith even as small as a mustard seed, you could say to this mountain, 'Move from here to there,' and it would move. Nothing would be impossible."

MATTHEW 17:20 NLT

I've seen a mustard seed, Lord! They're teensy-tiny, so small I could barely pick one up with my fingertips. So delicate they could fly right out of my hand, and I wouldn't even know it.

How many times have I used the excuse that my faith isn't big enough? That I'm not strong enough? You say I only need a tiny bit of faith and mountains can be moved. Today I offer You what I have, microscopic as it might seem. Thank You for moving the mountains in my life with my tiny offering of faith. Amen.

How big is a mustard seed?

I Know You're Listening

The LORD is far from the wicked, but he
hears the prayer of the righteous.
PROVERBS 15:29 ESV

It's remarkable to think that You can hear my prayers, Lord. I don't even have to speak them out loud, yet You hear them as if I've shouted them in Your ear!

Me, on the other hand? I don't always hear so well. Sometimes You whisper things to my heart and I miss them altogether. I'm so glad You never miss the prayers of Your people. I'm so grateful for Your consideration of my every need. May I never take Your attention for granted, Lord. I will walk with confidence, knowing You hear me. Amen.

Do you ever feel like your prayers are hitting the ceiling?
How do you get past those feelings to the truth?

I Trust You

Trust in the LORD with all your heart; do not depend on your own understanding. Seek his will in all you do, and he will show you which path to take.

PROVERBS 3:5-6 NLT

𝒴ou ask me to trust You with my whole heart. Not just pieces of it but every nook and cranny. Every hidden pocket. Every secret chamber.

Trusting You this way is not as easy as it sounds, Lord! How many times have I placed my trust in myself or kept things from You? How many times have I placed my trust in money or my job or other people instead of taking my concerns to the One who loves me most?

Today I choose to put You first. I will trust You above all. You are the Faithful One, and You love me passionately. I can trust You, Lord. Fully. That knowledge brings great peace to my soul. Amen.

*Who (or what) do you put your
trust in when troubles come?*

I Will Be Still

*He says, "Be still, and know that I am God; I will be
exalted among the nations, I will be exalted in the earth."*
PSALM 46:10 NIV

You will be exalted among the nations. What a remarkable
thought, Lord! Every city in every country on every
continent will come to know You. Every human being will
one day bow the knee to You. Until that day, You ask me to be
still and to trust—to know in my heart that You are Lord of all.

You are Lord of those cities. You are Lord of those
countries. You are Lord of those continents. You are Lord of
this planet and, indeed, of the whole universe! How could I
not trust the One who holds the entire world in His hands. I
do, Lord! I trust You from now through eternity. Amen.

Is "stillness" hard for you?

Anointed and Appointed

*"Before I formed you in the womb I knew
you, before you were born I set you apart;
I appointed you as a prophet to the nations."*
JEREMIAH 1:5 NIV

How I love this verse, Lord! You not only anointed me before I was born—You've appointed me as well. You have an assignment for me. Many of them, in fact!

This verse clues me in to a special secret: You set Your plans for me in motion before I even existed. Even then I was anointed to do great things for You! And I am appointed at this time in history to reach a certain group of people with the Gospel message. Wow!

How can I help but feel confident when I realize You went to such efforts to get me ready? Why would my knees ever knock? You have plans, and they are big ones! Your provision for me is staggering, really!

Let's do this, Lord! Amen.

Do you sense God's anointing and appointing in your life?

The Big Picture

Yet God has made everything beautiful for its own time. He has planted eternity in the human heart, but even so, people cannot see the whole scope of God's work from beginning to end.

ECCLESIASTES 3:11 NLT

*Y*ou make everything beautiful in its time, Lord. If it's not beautiful. . .it's not time. The fulfillment has not yet come. If it's not beautiful, I'll keep waiting until it is. If it's not beautiful, I'll keep trusting that one day it will be.

You see the big picture, far beyond what these earthly eyes can make out. You see the beauty in my mess. All I see is chaos and confusion, but You know what's ahead. You see the whole scope from beginning to end. I can walk with confidence, knowing You see it all. How wonderful to walk out Your plans in faith, knowing the outcome will be beautiful! Amen.

Are you a "big picture" person, or do you have trouble seeing the big picture?

You're Working It Out

*We know that God makes all things work
together for the good of those who love Him
and are chosen to be a part of His plan.*

ROMANS 8:28 NLV

Sometimes I feel like all I ever do is work. From the moment I get up in the morning to the time I rest my head on my pillow at night, I'm on the go.

It doesn't seem fair at times if I'm being honest. Then I'm reminded of how hard You work! You go 24-7 (not that You're limited by time, Lord, but You get the point). You never stop. You're working on my behalf even now! And You are working all things together for my good, which lets me know that my welfare is on Your mind at all times. My heart overflows with gratitude. Thanks for working so hard, Lord! Amen.

*Is it easy or hard for you to remember that
God is eventually going to work things out?*

It's Like This, Lord...

If we confess our sins, he is faithful and just to forgive
us our sins and to cleanse us from all unrighteousness.
1 JOHN 1:9 ESV

You have asked me to come to You and confess my sins, Lord. I don't always do that. Sometimes I just try to get away with them and hope You don't notice.

Why would I ever doubt Your kindness? You're not going to slap me down when I tell You what I've done. It's not like You don't already know all about it, anyway! But You have asked me to confess, not for Your sake but for my own. I am cleansed and purified as I lay my sins at Your feet. And then I'm free to rise up and walk in confidence, fully forgiven.

Today I come, ready to get a few things off my chest. Here goes, Lord! Amen.

Is it easier for you to confess to God or to people?

Coming with Confidence

*Let us then with confidence draw near to the
throne of grace, that we may receive mercy
and find grace to help in time of need.*

HEBREWS 4:16 ESV

There have been times, Lord, when the little ones in my world have come to me with heads bowed low, eyes shifted to the ground. They were so filled with shame over what they had done that they couldn't even look me in the eye.

I know that feeling well! How many times have I come to You with my gaze shifted downward? Far too many to count, such is the shame I've borne. You've asked me to come with confidence no matter what burdens I carry, no matter what sins I've committed. When I come confidently, You offer mercy and grace. What a good God you are!

Today, Lord. . .I come. Amen.

Are you intimidated by God's presence?

You Make Me Worthy

To this end we always pray for you, that our God may
make you worthy of his calling and may fulfill every
resolve for good and every work of faith by his power.

2 THESSALONIANS 1:11 ESV

. . . .

I have struggled with feelings of unworthiness my whole
life, Lord. Perhaps these feelings came about as a result of
how I was spoken to as a child. Or maybe I have just carried
so much guilt and shame that I couldn't imagine how You
could see me as anything other than intrinsically flawed.

My heart fills with joy as I realize that I am made worthy
through the blood of Your Son, Jesus, on the cross. Because of
His free gift of grace, worthiness is mine for the taking. I can
enter Your chambers boldly, confidently, not because of my
goodness, but because of His. How grateful I am for salvation
in Him, Lord! I've been made worthy in Your sight. Amen.

. . . .

Do you feel worthy?

You Live in Me

*I have been crucified with Christ and I no longer
live, but Christ lives in me. The life I now live
in the body, I live by faith in the Son of God,
who loved me and gave himself for me.*

GALATIANS 2:20 NIV

This is such a fascinating verse, Lord! You tell me that I have been crucified with Christ. What a concept! The old me is dead and gone. (Bye-bye, old me!) The sins of yesterday? Wiped away to exist no more.

Because of what Jesus did on the cross, I have a brand-new life. It's a life of faith. It's a life of gratitude. It's a life of hopeful possibilities. The death I have experienced was a necessary part of my journey with You, Lord, a transition from one world to another. I can hardly wait to thank You in person! Amen.

What does it mean to lay down your life?

I Call, You Answer!

He will call on me, and I will answer him; I will be with him in trouble, I will deliver him and honor him.

PSALM 91:15 NIV

. . . .

*P*eople don't always respond when I call them, Lord. Sometimes the phone will ring but nobody picks up. It's the same with my pets. When they're being naughty, I call out to them, but they hide under the bed to avoid my stern gaze.

You, though? You *always* answer. You want me to call. In fact, You're sitting by the phone right now, waiting! There's no incessant ringing when I dial Your number! You pick up immediately. You listen patiently, and then, sometimes to my surprise, You respond. You give me answers for all I'm facing. It's a two-way conversation laced with love.

How I love our chats. I'll be calling again soon, Lord! Amen.

. . . .

Do you consider your prayer time to be a two-way street?

The Best Is Yet to Come

*For I consider that the sufferings of this
present time are not worth comparing
with the glory that is to be revealed to us.*
ROMANS 8:18 ESV

I've had some pretty amazing adventures in this life,
Lord. You've taken me places I never dreamed I would
go, both in the natural and in the spiritual. Have I mentioned
how grateful I am?

When I look ahead, I can see that You have even bigger
things in store! I'm so curious. . .if the best is yet to come,
then what's out there for me? I guess I'll just have to take it
one day at a time and see for myself.

As I walk it out, I lay down any need to know the details.
I push my worries aside. All stresses disappear with the wind
as I place my trust in You. What fun this will be, Lord! I'm
ready if You are! Amen.

What does it mean to live with a sense of anticipation?

Prayer Will Take Us There

Therefore confess your sins to each other and pray
for each other so that you may be healed. The prayer
of a righteous person is powerful and effective.

JAMES 5:16 NIV

. . . .

*P*rayer is the vehicle to get me from point A to point
B, isn't it, Lord? In some ways it's kind of like a car or
plane. I wouldn't "wish" myself from one city to another (or
one country to another). I would get in a vehicle or board a jet.

I can't just wish and hope that my life will get better. I
have to actually reach out to You, talk to You, get into that
proverbial "vehicle" and be moved from my current situation
to wherever You are leading me next.

So today, Lord? I open the door to spend time with You.
I can hardly wait to see where You're taking me next. Let's
go! Amen.

. . . .

How powerful are your prayers?

By the Power of Your Spirit

*Our hope comes from God. May He fill you with joy
and peace because of your trust in Him. May your
hope grow stronger by the power of the Holy Spirit.*

ROMANS 15:13 NLV

The power of Your Spirit is what gives me energy. The power of Your Spirit breathes new life into these bones. Through Your Spirit, I can do things I never dreamed I could do. I can overcome obstacles. I can conquer foes. I can go above and beyond anything I dared to imagine.

My hope comes only from You, not from me. I don't have to depend on my own power, thank goodness! I would be in a lot of trouble, wouldn't I? No, I will rely solely on You, Father. Shower me with Your power today, I pray. Amen.

Where does your hope come from?

Supernatural Strength

He gives strength to the weary and
increases the power of the weak.
ISAIAH 40:29 NIV

I love the word *supernatural*, Lord. Anything You offer me is above and beyond this natural world. Your imagination? I can't even begin to fathom the things that go on in Your mind. Your love for me? It amazes me too! Your grace? Wow! So far beyond what I could imagine!

Your best gifts are *all* supernatural. So why would I doubt that You can empower me with supernatural strength? If You can give me hope, if You can give me peace, if You can supernaturally infuse me with joy, then I can count on You to give me strength for the journey, the kind that comes straight from Your throne to my weary body. It's supernatural! Amen.

Are you having to rely on God's
supernatural strength today?

To Love Deeply

Above all, love each other deeply,
because love covers over a multitude of sins.

1 Peter 4:8 NIV

. . . .

I'll confess that I don't always love others as I should, Lord. Perhaps some of the stresses in my life have come about because I'm going through the motions instead of genuinely, deeply caring about the situations of those around me. Maybe I don't really care as much as I should or I feel taken advantage of when they involve me.

Would You help me with my attitude? Give me Your heart for those You have placed in my life, a love that covers a multitude of sins. Give me compassion. Give me patience. Give me the right words to say when it's time to minister to them. Most of all, make me a reflection of You to the people in my world. I want to represent You well, Lord. Amen.

. . . .

Can you think of a time when God's love
covered a multitude of your own sins?

Your Ways Are Higher

"For my thoughts are not your thoughts,
neither are your ways my ways, declares the LORD."
ISAIAH 55:8 ESV

Sometimes I meet people who seem so far above me in their thinking. College professors. People with brilliant minds. I listen to them talk, and I'm overwhelmed trying to figure them out!

Your thoughts are even higher than theirs, Lord! All of the earthly knowledge can't come close to what You know. So when I wonder why things in my life aren't going according to my plan, I'll trust that You—the One with the highest thoughts and ways of all—are working out something far bigger, far greater than my finite mind could dream up.

I'm excited to see what You have for me as I journey forward, Lord. Thank You for working out big plans for me. Amen.

What would it be like to think like God?

You Will Give Me Rest

*"Come to me, all you who are weary
and burdened, and I will give you rest."*
MATTHEW 11:28 NIV

. . . .

I'm seeing this verse in a new light today, Lord. I see now
that rest is a gift from You. It's something You "give" me,
not something that just happens. When I consider it through
that lens, my entire approach to rest changes. I don't have to
wonder why rest doesn't come easily to me. I see the reason
in the first part of the verse. It's because I'm not coming to
You when I'm weary and burdened.

No wonder I get burned out. No wonder I always reach
the breaking point. You're right there, ready to hand me
the antidote, but I have to humble myself and come to You.
Today, Lord, I choose to do just that. Oh, how I long for Your
supernatural rest! Amen.

. . . .

Does resting come naturally to you?

Abounding in Hope

I lift up my eyes to the mountains—where does my help come from? My help comes from the LORD, the Maker of heaven and earth.
PSALM 121:1-2 NIV

I look up, Lord. Up to You. Up to hope. Up to the future. Up to great things ahead.

When life is tough—and I'll admit, it often is—my tendency is to look down. To give up. But no more! I'm shifting my gaze to the heavens because that's where my help, my hope, comes from. You are in charge of the universe and in charge of my life—every teensy-tiny bit of it—and I can trust You with it all.

So I'll look up and keep my focus on You, not on the circumstances swirling around me. They're nothing but a distraction, Lord. You are the immovable Rock. Thank You for holding steady. Amen.

Are you overflowing with hope today?

Pressing On

*Not that I have already obtained this or am
already perfect, but I press on to make it my
own, because Christ Jesus has made me his own.*
PHILIPPIANS 3:12 ESV

I'm thinking of a time I tried to run on the beach, Lord.
That loose sand was beautiful, but it sure made running
difficult. I felt bogged down. Held back. Unable to move at
my usual pace.

Sometimes I feel like that with the circumstances I face.
They're just too much for me. I get bogged down in them. I
can't put my finger on what's wrong, but it just feels like I'm
not free to run, to soar, in the usual way.

Then You step in and offer a word of encouragement.
I'm off and running again, ready to press on until I reach the
goal. Thank You for giving me the courage to keep going,
even when I don't feel like it. Amen.

When do you struggle the most with pressing on?

A Different Lens

For we walk by faith, not by sight.
2 CORINTHIANS 5:7 ESV

I'm figuring it out, Lord—there are two ways to view life: with my physical eyes and with my spiritual eyes. Moving forward according to what I can see with my physical eyes is tempting. That's the way modern culture thinks I should move. But life with You is a faith journey. It's a thrilling, trail-blazing adventure filled with opportunity after opportunity to impact the world if I will just do things Your way.

So I'll use a different lens to move forward from here, Lord. I'll do my best to walk by faith, not by sight. Thanks for leading and guiding when I can't see what's coming. Amen.

Which lens are you looking through—
your circumstances or your faith?

I'll Take Every Thought Captive

*We demolish arguments and every pretension that sets
itself up against the knowledge of God, and we take
captive every thought to make it obedient to Christ.*

2 CORINTHIANS 10:5 NIV

. . . .

I've been in situations where I felt trapped, Lord. In
those moments, I felt like a prisoner in a cage, unable
to break free.

You're asking me to take my thoughts captive in much
the same way. To see them bound up, tied down, unable to
move to the right or the left. Unable to rule me in any way.
You don't want my emotions to outweigh my faith. You're
calling me to a higher way of living.

So I'll take my thoughts captive. Only then will the
stresses I'm facing quiet down. Only then will I rise above
my circumstances and walk with hope, peace, and joy. Help
me, Lord, I pray. Amen.

. . . .

Do you struggle with discouraging or negative thoughts?

The Desires of My Heart

*May he give you the desire of your heart
and make all your plans succeed.*

PSALM 20:4 NIV

*Y*ou want to meet my needs, Lord. I'm so grateful. But there have been times I was scared to ask You for what I wanted because I felt I didn't deserve it. Or maybe I felt I didn't really need it.

This verse is startling to me! I read it, and I'm overwhelmed that You actually *want* me to be more detailed with You when I pray. You don't just long to meet my needs; You want to give me the desires of my heart. How deeply You must love me! Thank You for caring so much about the longings of my heart. You bring me such joy, Father! Amen.

*What are the desires of your heart at this very moment?
Are you going to make them known to the Lord?*

My Strength Forever

*My flesh and my heart may fail, but God is the
strength of my heart and my portion forever.*

PSALM 73:26 NIV

Just enough and just in time. That's the kind of God You
are. You give me what I need exactly when I need it, not
a moment before and never too late!

Sometimes I feel like You're not going to come through for
me, but You always do. I'll be honest, there are times when I'm
waiting with bated breath—hoping, praying, believing. . .but
often harboring a smidgen of doubt that things will turn out.

Then You show up! You infuse me with strength in the
waiting. You give me my "portion" of hope, and I'm able to
keep hanging on, even when it makes no sense to hang on.
You're my strength and portion forever, Lord. I won't give
up. Amen.

*What changes would you need to make to
walk in God's supernatural, eternal strength?*

Transcendent Peace

And the peace of God, which transcends all understanding,
will guard your hearts and your minds in Christ Jesus.
PHILIPPIANS 4:7 NIV

• •

It's inexplicable, Lord! Your peace transcends everything. It's an ethereal cloud hovering over me and enveloping me just when I'm about to panic. Your supernatural peace settles deep in my heart, and my attitude begins to shift. Stress fades. Calm settles over me.

I don't understand Your ways sometimes, Father, but that's part of the beauty of walking with You. I don't have to get it. I just have to trust, in spite of what I don't understand. And I have to walk in the assurance that You'll guard both my heart (which is shaky at best) and my mind (which tends to flitter all over the place). I do trust You, Lord. Thank You for the peace to keep on believing. Amen.

• •

What does "transcendent" peace look like to you?

One Day I'll See More Clearly

Now that which we see is as if we were looking in a broken mirror. But then we will see everything. Now I know only a part. But then I will know everything in a perfect way. That is how God knows me right now.

1 CORINTHIANS 13:12 NLV

The scene in front of me is blurry sometimes, Lord—like I'm wearing someone else's glasses with a prescription that's far different from my own. I can't make out the pathway. The story makes no sense. I can't see where You're taking me. . .or how I'm going to get from point A to point B.

Still, You call me to trust in You. This broken image will one day be made clear. Right now You're showing me just enough to increase my faith and give me the wherewithal to keep putting one foot in front of the other. It's not easy. I get scared. But I won't stop. Guide me step by step, I pray. Amen.

Are you looking forward to the day when all will be made clear?

Power, Love, and Self-Discipline

For the Spirit God gave us does not make us timid,
but gives us power, love and self-discipline.

2 TIMOTHY 1:7 NIV

Lord, You've given me everything I need to make it through any tough circumstance. Your Word promises power, love, and self-discipline. A person can go a long way on those three things.

You offer fortitude. I need this supernatural inside-out power to get through the tasks in front of me. I need courage to stop these knees from knocking. I need tenacity to keep going, even when I don't feel like it. And I need self-discipline to stay committed to the tasks in front of me.

You promise it all! And in the process, You'll also give me boldness so that I'm not afraid as I step forward into the great unknown. Thank You, Lord! Amen.

Do you truly believe that God didn't make you timid?

Whatever I Ask For

"Therefore I tell you, whatever you ask for in prayer,
believe that you have received it, and it will be yours."

MARK 11:24 NIV

*W*ow, what a promise, Lord! You've said in Your Word that if my faith is strong enough, I can receive whatever I ask for. I have some big things on my list and wonder how far I should take this! Should I believe for the impossible? That child who has wandered from You? That financial situation that seems too big to fix? That coworker who grates on my nerves?

I should bring all of that to You? (Oh, that's right—it was Your idea, not mine!) I'll up my faith, Lord. I'll begin to think bigger, to trust deeper, and to ask with more intention. Only when I increase my faith will I see miracles happen. I'm ready, Lord! Amen.

"Whatever" can mean different things to
different people. What does it mean to you?

Our Safe Place

Trust in Him at all times, O people. Pour out your heart before Him. God is a safe place for us.

PSALM 62:8 NLV

So many times I've wished for a friend to tell my troubles to. Someone who would listen and not butt in. Someone who would genuinely care but not overwhelm me with their ideas and plans to fix my problem. Then I'm reminded that You've been there all along.

You're the best place to run, Lord. You provide safety, compassion, comfort, and gentle wisdom. I can count on You to give the best advice, even in situations where I'm completely overwhelmed. So I'll tell You my troubles. (Thanks for listening!) And I know You'll have solutions to every problem I face, so I'll lean in close to hear what You're whispering in my ear. Amen.

Where do you usually run for safety?

You Delight in My Well-Being

May those who delight in my vindication shout for joy and gladness; may they always say, "The LORD be exalted, who delights in the well-being of his servant."
PSALM 35:27 NIV

You care about every intricate part of me, Lord—from my trembling hands to my knocking knees. You care when I'm having a good day, and You're fully tuned in when I'm having a bad one. You delight in my well-being, so You're working overtime to make sure I've got what it takes to see this thing through. Even when my enemies are chasing me down, I have nothing to fear. You're right there, ready to come out swinging on my behalf.

Good days or bad, rough situations or smooth, I put my trust in You. My allies will shout victoriously when You come through for me. I can hardly wait for that day! Amen.

Why do you suppose God delights in our well-being?

I'll Keep Going

Let us not grow weary of doing good, for in
due season we will reap, if we do not give up.
GALATIANS 6:9 ESV

• •

I want to give up. Seriously. I'm just not feeling it today, Lord. My "want-to" has flown out the window. It would be easier to do nothing than to put one foot in front of the other.

Then I think about all You went through for me. Your Son put one foot in front of the other on His walk to Calvary, didn't He? You put one (proverbial) foot in front of the other when You raised Him from the grave. How then can I balk at doing good things for You? I'll keep going, even on the days when I'm not feeling it. Why? Because You did, Lord, and I'm a reflection of You! Amen.

• •

How do you keep going when you don't feel like it?

I Put My Hope in You

*Why, my soul, are you downcast? Why so
disturbed within me? Put your hope in God,
for I will yet praise him, my Savior and my God.*

PSALM 42:11 NIV

. . . .

I love this verse so much, Lord! It reminds me of the many times I've talked to myself: "Self, what's wrong with you? Why do you keep messing up? Soul, why are you so downcast? What are you so worked up about? Have you really forgotten that the God of the universe is on Your side and is working on your behalf?"

This verse reminds me to place my trust in You, Lord, which is where it belongs. I put my hope in You and praise You even now because You're a trustworthy God. You've never let me down, and You won't start now! Amen.

. . . .

*When you're down in the dumps,
what do you do to turn things around?*

Overflowing

*You are making a table of food ready for me in
front of those who hate me. You have poured
oil on my head. I have everything I need.*

PSALM 23:5 NLV

I love how You work, Lord! You don't just protect and
guard me from my enemies; You make a show out of how
much You love me. . .in front of them! You prepare a table
before me in the presence of those who are out to get me. You
want them to know You're on my side. And You spread out a
feast—the finest foods, the most expensive wines. You lavish
oil on my head, giving me peace, even when my enemies are
staring me down from across the room.

I won't worry with You on my side, Lord. I have everything
I need and more. How grateful I am for Your overflowing
provision! Amen.

*Why would God prepare a table before
you in the presence of your enemies?*

By the Power of Your Spirit

May the God of hope fill you with all joy
and peace as you trust in him, so that you may
overflow with hope by the power of the Holy Spirit.
ROMANS 15:13 NIV

• •

I'll admit it, Lord: I'm not always overflowing with hope. More often than not a leak has sprung in the bottom of my proverbial boat, and I feel like I'm sinking instead of overflowing.

Today I ask for what feels impossible—hope, joy, and peace—as I place my trust in You. I know Your Word says this is possible, and I definitely need a change of thinking about my situation, so I'm going to give it a try! I want to overflow with hope by the power of Your Spirit, Lord. Do what only You can do. Turn my situation—and my heart—around, I pray. Amen.

• •

Where does your hope come from?

Great Understanding

Whoever is patient has great understanding,
but one who is quick-tempered displays folly.

PROVERBS 14:29 NIV

Sometimes my temper gets the best of me, Lord. I flare up and then wonder why my heart is racing and my hands are trembling. I can get hyped up in a hurry, for sure!

Today I'm asking You to calm the tumultuous seas. Do what only You can do. Turn this sometimes-erratic overreactor into a calm, patient person You can be proud of. I want to represent You well in this life, Lord. You're not flipping out, so I don't need to either.

Replace my quick temper with a steady commitment to You—Your way, Your plan. Rid me of folly, and make me a good example to others, I pray. Amen.

Would people say that you're quick-tempered?

I Won't Give Up

Do not let yourselves get tired of doing good. If we do not give up, we will get what is coming to us at the right time.
GALATIANS 6:9 NLV

. . . .

I want to throw in the towel. I really do, Lord. I'm done. Finished. Kaput. I've had it. I'm not taking another step forward. Only You won't let me quit, will You? You have this thing about plowing forward even when I don't feel like it. You tell me that I can finish what I've started if I fight the temptation to give up.

It's not going to be easy, but I'll give this endeavor another shot. Obviously, I can't do it on my own, so I'm placing my trust in You, Lord. I'll trust Your timing and Your strength, in Jesus' mighty name. Amen.

. . . .

How do you feel knowing good things are coming
at just the right time if you don't give up?

Ask, Seek, Knock

*"Ask, and it will be given to you; seek, and you
will find; knock, and it will be opened to you."*

MATTHEW 7:7 ESV

Lord, You've told me to ask. . .so I'm asking. There are so many needs in my life right now. I want to bring them straight to You because I know You're the only One with any answers. You told me to seek, so I'm seeking—Your will, Your way, Your plan, not my own. You've told me to knock, and here I stand, knocking at Your door. Swing it wide, I pray. Usher me in so that not one moment is wasted doing things the world's way. (I tried the world's way, Lord, and it only led to stress and chaos.)

Your plan is simple: come to You. So today I choose to bring You every concern, every wish, every problem, and every dream. I lay them at Your feet, Father, and ask You to do with them as You will. Amen.

*How are asking, seeking, and knocking
different from each other?*

Refreshed

*He refreshes my soul. He guides me along
the right paths for his name's sake.*

PSALM 23:3 NIV

• •

I love that "just washed" feeling after taking a shower. It feels wonderful to be cleansed, refreshed, readied for the day ahead.

In many ways, this is the same feeling I have after spending time with You, Lord. I enter into a time of renewal. My weary soul is bathed in Your love. I come away ready to face whatever life throws my way. Thank You for refreshing me. Thank You for giving me the wherewithal to keep moving along life's paths. Amen.

• •

*Where is God guiding you during
this current season you're in?*

You're More Than Able

Now to him who is able to do immeasurably more than all we ask or imagine, according to his power that is at work within us, to him be glory in the church and in Christ Jesus throughout all generations, for ever and ever! Amen.

EPHESIANS 3:20–21 NIV

• •

There's no ruler to gauge how deep Your love is for me, Lord. There's no measuring tape to calculate the distance from the cross to the empty tomb. But I know this about You: You would go any distance to reach me. You always do more than I expect. You give more than I think You will. You're an "above and beyond" Creator, working on my behalf at all times out of Your great love for me.

I praise You, Father, for this overwhelming, immeasurable love. It's so much more than I could ever ask or think. How grateful I am. Amen.

• •

What does "immeasurably" mean to you?

Wounds Healed

"I will give you back your health and heal your wounds," says the LORD. "For you are called an outcast—'Jerusalem for whom no one cares.'"
JEREMIAH 30:17 NLT

Some of the wounds in my life have run deep, Lord. They haven't been the kind people could see with their eyes, but they were there all the same. They kept me doubled over in pain, and healing never seemed to come.

Then You stepped in! In an instant, You did what I couldn't do in years of trying. You brought healing and wholeness. You restored me, replenishing my hope, my joy, and my peace. I was an outcast no more. I was made whole, thanks to Your great love. Oh, what joy to live a healed life. Amen.

What healing has God brought to Your life?

You Are Greater

*You, dear children, are from God and have
overcome them, because the one who is in you
is greater than the one who is in the world.*

1 JOHN 4:4 NIV

Sometimes I feel so small and inadequate, Lord. I get overwhelmed too easily. In those moments, my perspective is skewed. I look at tiny hills and call them mountains. They loom in front of me like Mount Everest.

But You, Lord? You're bigger than all of them! No matter how large a problem, You're greater still. And You've given me the power to overcome even the biggest foe!

Change my perspective, I pray. Instead of focusing on all the reasons I can't, I want to zero in on the fact that You can. . .and You will. I have nothing to fear as long as my perspective is right, Lord! Amen.

Who is "the one who is in the world"?

Committed and Established

Commit to the LORD whatever you do,
and he will establish your plans.

PROVERBS 16:3 NIV

• •

*L*ord, this verse reminds me of the many times in school when I was asked to sign a commitment form. When I put my name on the dotted line, I was making a promise—that I would follow my words with actions. I would commit and would follow through no matter how I felt or how many distractions came my way.

That's what You long from me too. You want my whole heart, every piece of it. When I say yes to You, I'm saying yes for the long haul, not just when I feel like it. I'll remain committed, dedicated, fully on board, no matter what distractions come my way. And I'll enjoy the fruit of my labors when all is said and done as You establish Your plans in my life. Amen.

• •

What active steps can you take to
commit yourself to the Lord today?

Happy in You

Be happy in the Lord. And He will
give you the desires of your heart.
PSALM 37:4 NLV

∙∙∙

I'm learning that happiness is a choice, Lord. I can choose to be happy in You even when circumstances cry out, "Give up! Give in to despair!"

I won't give in. I'll make the right choice. And when I do, You will give me the desires of my heart. Honestly? This verse makes me wonder how many times I had to wait for the desires of my heart because I chose despair instead of faith.

I'll be happy. I'll choose joy. And I'll anticipate Your miraculous intervention followed by a marvelous outpouring of Your compassion and love. Amen.

∙∙∙

What are the desires of your heart?

God of the Impossible

"What do you mean, 'If I can'?" Jesus asked.
"Anything is possible if a person believes."

MARK 9:23 NLT

If it feels completely impossible to me, Lord, I know You're not feeling that way. In fact, the more impossible it seems, the more I'm forced to depend on You.

There's no need to ask if You can, Lord. I know You can. You're capable of parting the seas, toppling walls, and putting broken lives back together. And You tell me that anything is possible if I will just believe.

So I'm tossing my "impossibles," Lord! With You, nothing is impossible. I'll wait with fervent faith to see how You turn this situation around. And until then, I'll keep on hoping, keep on believing, and keep on speaking in faith. Amen.

What feels impossible to you right now?

Strategies for Relational Healing

*Be kind and compassionate to one another, forgiving
each other, just as in Christ God forgave you.*
EPHESIANS 4:32 NIV

I love when the pieces of a broken relationship come back together quickly, Lord! You can certainly mend broken hearts and put the pieces back together in a hurry. Other times the healing seems to take forever. I start to wonder if things will ever be right again.

In the gap in between—before true relational healing comes—You've asked for my participation: to be kind, compassionate, and forgiving. I know that exhibiting this kind of attitude will help mend the broken places, so I'll do my best, Father. I'll go on loving even if the other person makes it difficult. I'll offer forgiveness even if they don't ask, because You forgave me. After all, I've experienced firsthand the power of forgiveness. How could I help but offer it to others?

Thank You for mending broken relationships, Lord! Amen.

What does it mean to forgive as Christ forgave you?

Living Wisely

Be very careful, then, how you live—not as unwise but as wise, making the most of every opportunity, because the days are evil.

EPHESIANS 5:15–16 NIV

. . . .

I'll admit it, Lord! Sometimes (okay, *many* times) I don't think before I leap. I make quick, impulsive decisions or choices and then live to regret them.

You want me to make wisdom my BFF, to give it a permanent room in my home. I won't have anything to regret after the fact if I allow Your wisdom to lead me. Best of all, I can live stress-free if I choose wisdom every time. I won't give way to the enemy (that roaring lion). I won't let him bring me down. No, not anymore! I'm on to him. I'm done falling into his trap. Wisdom lives in my house! Thank You for giving it to me as a gift. Amen.

. . . .

How do you keep your spiritual antennae up during these precarious days?

I Trust You, Lord

But those who trust in the LORD will find new strength.
They will soar high on wings like eagles. They will run
and not grow weary. They will walk and not faint.

ISAIAH 40:31 NLT

I wonder why I'm zapped. I wonder why I feel like I'm running on empty. Then I realize I've shifted my trust—from You to me. I didn't do it on purpose, Lord, but it happened.

It's time to turn this situation around, but I'm going to need Your help. I'm tired of relying on myself! I want to rise up from my weariness to soar high on wings like eagles, as Your Word says. So I place my trust in You. In You, I find energy to keep running the race without growing exhausted. I can walk—no matter how long it takes—and not faint.

Thank You for the joy You bring when I trust in You! Amen.

What does it mean to soar high on eagles' wings?

I'll Build Them Up

*Therefore encourage one another and build
each other up, just as in fact you are doing.*
1 THESSALONIANS 5:11 NIV

The world is filled with people who love to cut each other down. They can't wait to find flaws—in their loved ones, coworkers, even their closest friends.

Your Word tells us to have the opposite spirit—to encourage others and build them up. No limitation is placed on that command. Your Word doesn't say, "Only when they're behaving right," or "Only when they do what you want them to do." No, we're to offer encouragement and to build up others no matter how a situation is unpacking itself.

Building others up isn't always easy for me, Lord. I'll admit it. But with Your help, I'll become one of the best encouragers around. You've been that for me, after all! It's the least I can do in return. Amen.

What can you do today to build up those you love?

Your Divine Power

*His divine power has given us everything we need
for a godly life through our knowledge of him
who called us by his own glory and goodness.*

2 PETER 1:3 NIV

Sometimes I watch those superhero movies and wish I could have the kind of power they seem to possess. Watching all of the miraculous feats they perform is mind-blowing!

Then I remember that Your power is greater still. And You've shared that power with me! Your Word says that You've given me everything I need to get through this life. Everything, Lord? Wow! I might not be able to scale buildings in a single bound, but I can leap over problems and soar above challenges. I can speak to mountains and watch them fall in the name of Jesus!

You really have given me all I need, and I praise You today for calling me to a life of power! Amen.

What has God's divine power given you?

Glory Is Coming!

For I consider that the sufferings of this present time are not worth comparing with the glory that is to be revealed to us.

ROMANS 8:18 ESV

. . . .

*I*n the light of eternity." How I love these words! The things I'm fretting over today—the very things I've lost sleep over—won't matter at all when I get to heaven. I won't even remember them.

Until then, please help me keep things in perspective, Lord. Your perspective. When it comes to the non-eternal things, help me to push them aside in my mind so that I'm not fixated on them. Only when I do so will I really rise above my circumstances to walk a faith-filled life with You. I can't wait to spend eternity with You, Lord! Amen.

. . . .

Have you ever pondered eternity?

Scripture Index

OLD TESTAMENT

NEW TESTAMENT

MORE INSPIRATION FOR
Your Beautiful Soul

Choose Joy: 3-Minute Devotions for Women 978-1-63409-998-1

Choose Prayer: 3-Minute Devotions for Women 978-1-68322-398-6

Choose Grace: 3-Minute Devotions for Women 978-1-68322-255-2

Choose Hope: 3-Minute Devotions for Women 978-1-68322-174-6

Got 3 minutes to spare? You'll find the spiritual pick-me-up you crave in these inspiring 3-minute devotionals. Written especially for the twenty-first-century woman, these delightful books pack a powerful dose of comfort, encouragement, and hope into just-right-sized readings. Minute 1: scripture to meditate on; Minute 2: a short devotional reading; Minute 3: a prayer to jump-start a conversation with God.

Paperback / $4.99 each